ERASMUS, UTOPIA, AND THE JESUITS

ERASMUS, UTOPIA, AND THE JESUITS
Essays on the Outreach of Humanism

by
JOHN C. OLIN

Fordham University Press
New York
1994

Copyright © 1994 by John C. Olin
All rights reserved
LC 94-27440
ISBN 0-8232-1600-4 (hardcover)
ISBN 0-8232-1601-2 (paperback)

Library of Congress Cataloging-in-Publication Data
Olin, John C.
   Erasmus, utopia, and the Jesuits : essays on the outreach of humanism / John C. Olin.
      p.   cm.
   Includes bibliographical references.
   ISBN 0-8232-1600-4 (hard). — ISBN 0-8232-1601-2 (pbk.)
   1. Erasmus, Desiderius, d. 1536—Influence. 2. Humanism.
3. Utopias. 4. Jesuits—Education. I. Title.
B785.E64045   1994
001.3'09'031—dc20   94-27440
                                                              CIP

Printed in the United States of America

To
Marian
with love and gratitude

CONTENTS

List of Illustrations	ix
Abbreviations	xi
Introduction	xiii
1 Erasmus and Saint Jerome: The Close Bond and Its Significance	1
2 Erasmus and His Edition of Saint Hilary	27
3 Erasmus and Aldus Manutius	39
4 Erasmus' *Adagia* and More's *Utopia*	57
5 More, Montaigne, and Matthew Arnold: Thoughts on the Utopian Vision	71
6 The Jesuits, Humanism, and History	85

LIST OF ILLUSTRATIONS

Erasmus by Quentin Metsys of Louvain	facing p. 1
Saint Jerome in His Study by Antonio da Fabriano	3
Title page of the Aldine (1508) edition of Erasmus' *Adagia*.	50
Statue of Thomas More outside Chelsea Old Church	61
Saint Ignatius Loyola by Andrea Pozzo	87

ABBREVIATIONS

Allen   *Opus Epistolarum Des. Erasmi Roterodami*. Edd. P. S. Allen, H. M. Allen, and H. W. Garrod. 12 vols. Oxford, 1906–1958.

CHR[3]   *Christian Humanism and the Reformation: Selected Writings of Erasmus*. Ed. John C. Olin. 3rd ed. New York, 1987.

CWE   *Collected Works of Erasmus*. In progress. Toronto and Buffalo, 1974—.

HO   *Hieronymi Opera*. Ed. Erasmus. 9 vols. Basel, 1516.

HV   *Hieronymi Vita*. The composite text in *Erasmi Opuscula*. Ed. Wallace K. Ferguson. The Hague, 1933. Pp. 134–90.

INTRODUCTION

THE ESSAYS IN THIS VOLUME stem from my particular interests in the Renaissance and Reformation, specifically in the early decades of the sixteenth century which witnessed the juncture of those two movements. The terms are conventional, but they do signify historical events that can readily be defined, especially if our definitions are selective and reflect our own focus and point of view. By the Renaissance I mean the great interest in and study of the languages and literature of classical antiquity which characterized the period. There are other more specific names for this development—the New Learning, for example. That term distinguishes this important feature from the scholasticism of the Middle Ages and calls attention to a significant cultural shift or break with the past. Humanism is another term and has greater validity, being more closely associated with the actual event itself. The term derives from the Latin *humanitas*, one of whose meanings is the learning or intellectual cultivation that befits our humanity. In the Renaissance this was perceived as the result of an education based on the ancient classics, the *studia humanitatis*, as it was called, the studies most appropriate and beneficial in view of our human qualities and potential.

By virtue of all that it was, Renaissance humanism had a reform thrust. It stimulated intellectual ferment and cultural change. It put a new emphasis on man and his dignity. It believed that the revival of classical letters, the *litterae humaniores*, and an education based thereon would produce a better and more enlightened person. Moral as well as intellectual reform was a goal; religious and social reform would inevitably follow. This reform thrust is all the more understandable when one realizes that a scriptural and patristic revival was an integral part of Renaissance humanism. The latter embraced the languages and literature of Christian as well as pagan antiquity and represented a tradition closer to the thought of the early Church Fathers than to the Burckhardtian and once prevalent view of a revival of antiquity antithetical to Christianity.

These remarks help explain my approach to the Reformation and its connection with the Renaissance. I view that development in a very broad sense and not simply as a religious revolution that began with Luther and continued with Calvin. I think of it as including a wide array of efforts aimed at reform—personal, social, institutional—and I see it as a multi-faceted phenomenon that humanism played a major role in inspiring and guiding. Thus, the juncture of these two movements, the dynamic union of these two historical events. I hasten to add that other factors are most certainly involved in the story of the Renaissance and Reformation. History's checkered course is not so easily described. I have focused on one aspect, a very important one, but only one of several. I explain it here by way of introduction to the essays that follow and present it as an underlying theme which the essays for the most part will exemplify, clarify, and corroborate.

My first essay concerns Erasmus and Saint Jerome, the early Church Father whom the great humanist most highly esteemed and whose work he edited and published in a landmark edition in 1516.[1] I discuss the bond or affinity that existed between them and emphasize its humanistic character as well as Erasmus' ever-present reform goal. Without question the "prince of humanists" is the prime example of a humanist reformer. The second essay is about another of Erasmus' patristic editions, his edition of the writings of Saint Hilary of Poitiers which appeared in 1523. I examine in particular the dedicatory letter to Jean de Carondelet which prefaced it.[2] The letter is a major statement of Erasmus' point of view regarding the religious crisis that was now so serious. Both these essays deal with an important but long-neglected segment of Erasmus' humanist scholarship and stress its fundamental reform purpose.[3] The third essay centers on Erasmus' collaboration with the famous Venetian scholar-printer Aldus Manutius in 1508. It is an important episode in Erasmus' life and in the broader history of Renaissance humanism. A key edition of Erasmus' *Adagia* was published that year by the Aldine Press—which brings us to the fourth essay on the *Adagia* and Thomas More's *Utopia*. I link one of the proverbs Erasmus prominently expounds in his book, namely, "Friends have all things in common," with the theme of *Utopia*, and I claim that the two humanists are presenting the same moral and religious ideal, although in very different ways. In the fifth essay I continue the discussion of the utopian idea and describe several such projections found in famous literary works.[4] I begin with More's classic and end with a work of Matthew Arnold's, and I add a few summary observations about the utopian vision. The sixth and last essay treats Saint Ignatius Loyola and the early Jesuits and focuses on the humanistic character of their own studies and of the vast educational enterprise they established.[5] I make bold to say that this part of their apostolate is "one of the great extensions and consolidations of Renaissance humanism," and I conclude with some remarks about the meaning and relevance of such education today.

These essays are obviously linked by their common concern with humanism. Each treats an aspect of that movement—patristic scholarship, Erasmus and Aldus Manutius, *Utopia* and the utopian vision, the Jesuit educational enterprise—but they diverge somewhat from the usual treatment of Renaissance humanism, or, rather, they extend beyond the standard treatment so often confined to the classical revival. Hence, I subtitled the collection "Essays on the Outreach of Humanism." I wanted to underscore the character of the essays as well as highlight the broad range of humanism itself. In a sense the book is a sequel to an earlier collection of essays of mine, *Six Essays on Erasmus*, which Fordham University Press published in 1979, and complements or supplements that earlier work. I have noted companion essays in that volume which tie in with the entries in this present one, and I am struck by the consistency of tone and the continuity of theme that exist.

For the record let me indicate the provenance of these essays. The first one, "Erasmus and Saint Jerome," originally was the Erasmus of Rotterdam Society Birthday Lecture I delivered at the Folger Shakespeare Library in Washington on October 27, 1986, and it was subsequently published in the *Erasmus of Rotterdam Society Yearbook Seven (1987)*. The second, "Erasmus and His Edition of Saint Hilary," began as a paper I gave at a session of the American Historical Association's annual convention in Dallas on December 30, 1977, and it was published in the University of Toronto Press' *Erasmus in English*, 9 (1978). The third, "Erasmus and Aldus Manutius," I wrote for this volume. The fourth, "Erasmus' *Adagia* and More's *Utopia*," I contributed to the *Festschrift* for Abbé Germain Marc'hadour, *Miscellanea Moreana*, Moreana 100, edd. Clare M. Murphy, Henri Gibaud, and Mario A. Di Cesare (Binghamton, N.Y., 1989). The source of the fifth essay, "More, Montaigne, and Matthew Arnold," is a paper I gave at an international conference on Utopia in Sydney, Australia, July 10, 1992. The sixth essay, "The Jesuits, Humanism, and History," is based on a lecture I originally gave at John Carroll University in Cleveland on March 8, 1991, and at Fordham University, Lincoln Center, New York City, on April 10, 1991. It commemorates the 500th anniversary of the birth of Saint Ignatius Loyola. I thank those whose invitations initiated these essays, and I am particularly grateful to the Fordham University Press for encouraging me to collect them and prepare this volume. My long association with the Press has been one of the good fortunes and rewards of my academic life.

I would like to add that I have tried to compose these essays with some effort at readability and style. I have long subscribed to the dictum of George Macaulay Trevelyan's in his essay on "Clio, a Muse" that "history is not merely the accumulation and interpretation of facts—hard enough, that, in itself—but involves besides the whole art of book composition and prose style."[6] Such a double task has been a goal for me, and I hope I have not failed too badly on either score. There is another admonition that I have kept in mind and that I also want to quote. It comes from Ronald Knox, an author of considerable brilliance and versatility whom I have long admired. It is simply the obvious truth that "books are meant to be read, and the first quality of a book is that people shall read it and want to go on reading it."[7] That may be too ambitious a hope for essays such as these, but in writing them I have tried to some extent to reflect this awareness.

NOTES

1. See CWE 61, *Patristic Scholarship: The Edition of St. Jerome*, edd. James F. Brady and John C. Olin (Toronto, 1992).

2. The letter to Carondelet is in my *Six Essays on Erasmus* (New York, 1979), pp. 93–120, and in CWE 9, Letter 1334.

3. On Erasmus' patristic editions see my *Six Essays*, chap. 3, "Erasmus and the Church Fathers," pp. 33–47.

4. See also a companion essay of mine, "The Idea of Utopia from Hesiod to John Paul II," in *Interpreting Thomas More's* UTOPIA, ed. John C. Olin (New York, 1989), pp. 77–98.

5. See a companion essay, "Erasmus and St. Ignatius Loyola," in my *Six Essays*, chap. 6, pp. 75–92.

6. *Clio, a Muse, and Other Essays Literary and Pedestrian* (London, 1913), p. 34.

7. *On English Translation* (Oxford, 1957), p. 5. This is the Romanes Lecture which Knox delivered at Oxford in June 1957, shortly before he died.

ERASMUS, UTOPIA, AND THE JESUITS

Erasmus by Quentin Metsys of Louvain (at Hampton Court).
The Royal Collection © Her Majesty Queen Elizabeth II.

1

Erasmus and Saint Jerome: The Close Bond and Its Significance

I

IN THE WALTERS ART GALLERY in Baltimore there is a painting of Saint Jerome in his study by Antonio da Fabriano that is of particular interest. Save for the halo about the head of Jerome, it bears a striking resemblance to the Quentin Metsys portrait of Erasmus that was painted at Antwerp in 1517. The Fabriano painting dates from the mid-fifteenth century, but there is little likelihood that Metsys ever saw it or even knew of it. Fabriano's painting of Jerome in his study, of course, is neither an original nor a unique representation, and there is a long tradition of depicting authors and scholars in such a setting.[1] The similarity between the Metsys and the Fabriano portrayals, however, seems to me especially remarkable. Together the paintings vividly express, I feel, the close and intimate bond that existed between the two great Christian humanists, and they can serve, therefore, as a starting point—and an iconographic representation, if you will—for the subject I am going to discuss.

You are familiar, I know, with the Metsys portrait. The extremely pensive figure of Erasmus in black cloak and cap

---

Parts of this essay appear in the Introduction to CWE 61, *Patristic Scholarship: The Edition of St. Jerome*, edd. James F. Brady and John C. Olin (Toronto, 1992), a volume particularly relevant and supplementary to this essay.

in his study, writing at his desk in a large copy book, has often been reproduced. There are actually two copies of the painting—one, long thought to be the original, at the Galleria Nazionale d'Arte Antica in Rome, the other in the Royal Collection at Hampton Court.

Margaret Mann Phillips has suggested that the Hampton Court portrait may well be the original because of the handwriting in the copy book which closely resembles Erasmus'.[2] The Metsys portrait was also one part of a diptych (the other painting is a portrait of Pieter Gillis, town secretary at Antwerp) sent to Thomas More in September 1517. There are some other notable details in the Hampton Court portrait that are not found in the Roman one. In the wall behind Erasmus there are two shelves of books with three books lying on their side which are prominently labeled on their page ends: The New Testament, Lucian, Jerome. The triad practically comprises the main inspirations of Erasmus. The inscriptions are also titles of three important editions of his, the New Testament and the Jerome being landmark works that had appeared the preceding year. In the Hampton Court portrait there is also the legible handwriting in the book before Erasmus, who stands with pen in hand. There appears on the page he has just finished writing the heading and opening words of his Paraphrase of Saint Paul's Epistle to the Romans, a work published at Louvain that same year.

Antonio da Fabriano's portrayal of Saint Jerome in his study has a larger and busier background than the Metsys painting. Jerome's cardinal's hat hangs on a peg on the wall behind him, where there is also an archway opening to another room. The double shelf of books, however, is there within reach of the scholar, and Jerome is seated at his desk also with pen in hand writing in a large copy book. Although his dress is different and his head is capped by a gilded halo, his bearing and his visage are almost identical to Erasmus'. He too is pondering what he writes. There is an open book propped up on the desk to his left whose text apparently is

St. Jerome in his Study by Antonio da Fabriano (fifteenth century). Reproduced by permission of the Walters Art Gallery, Baltimore.

the subject of his thought, and a scroll of paper or parchment with writing on it hangs from the bookshelf just above it. A large hourglass holds it securely in place. It is the words of Holy Scripture which undoubtedly engross him, as they do Erasmus in the Metsys portrait. Jerome most probably is at work on a scriptural commentary or translation. Despite the halo, Fabriano has presented a thoroughly humanized Jerome—the dedicated scholar par excellence amidst the essential tools of his craft in the corner of a bright airy room. The conventional accouterments and the other iconographic symbols of a Jerome portrait are minimal. Aside from the books only the anachronistic cardinal's hat and the hourglass, which serves by the way a very useful purpose, are present. The painter's singleness of focus and relative simplicity of detail distinguish it, for example, from Albrecht Dürer's famous engraving of Saint Jerome in his study and link it more closely than any other comparable portrayal of Jerome with the Metsys portrait of Erasmus. But it is the appearance of the scholar-saint—his posture and mien—that most forcefully establishes the resemblance I have noted.

How meaningful is this resemblance? Obviously, the paintings give evidence of a similarity in the role and activity of their two subjects. Here are two serious scholars and authors totally engaged in their scholarly work. But the resemblance is a great deal more striking than that. Their work actually is identical, as is their deep concentration on the sacred text they ponder. Their pensive gaze is far from superficial; they seek to penetrate the word of God and translate and expound it. The same purpose inspires them, the same spirit moves them. Indeed, the Metsys portrait would seem to consciously reflect that kinship with Jerome that Erasmus himself perceived. The inscription "Hieronymus" so prominently displayed on the book end informs us as much. And the earlier Fabriano painting depicts a humanistic Jerome who serves as an exemplar for the Christian scholar and is a prototype of the prince of humanists still to come. The two paintings thus dramatically and impressively express an affinity that I now want to explore further.

II

That there was a humanist cult of Jerome as well as a more strictly devotional and religious one in the late medieval and Renaissance periods we know from the art and the literature of those times. Several studies have called this to our attention.[3] We know too that Erasmus from his early years knew Jerome as both saint and scholar. The Brethren of the Common Life with whom he had studied and lived as a child and young man were named *Hieronymiani* because of their devotion to Jerome, and P. S. Allen suggests that his interest in the saint stems from this association.[4] Even as a young canon at Steyn he had read and copied all the letters of Jerome and had drawn lessons from them which explain both his attachment to their author and his early formation as a humanist. A letter to a fellow Augustinian Cornelis Gerard, probably written in 1489, is most revealing in this regard.[5] He comments that if those who despise poetry and good writing "looked carefully at Jerome's letters, they would see that lack of culture is not holiness, nor cleverness impiety." Jerome's letters had become for him a literary treasure and an arsenal of arguments against the "barbarians' assaults," and drawing on Jerome as well as Saint Augustine he undertook to write a work against these opponents of good literature.[6] The judgments and views that will characterize Erasmus throughout his life have already begun to find expression. But Jerome was not his only model or inspiration. Erasmus is already well versed in the literature of antiquity, and he has discovered authors of his own time "who approach quite closely the ancient ideal of eloquence."[7] He is keenly aware of the renaissance of art and letters then taking place, and he credits Lorenzo Valla especially for refuting the "barbarians" and helping to restore good literature and style.

From the start, however, Jerome occupied a special place in Erasmus' studies and scholarly plans. By 1500, soon after his return to the continent from a memorable trip to England where he had met John Colet at Oxford and the young Thomas More, Erasmus went to work on a project to restore and edit the letters of Jerome and write a commentary on them. It is his first major enterprise. He had now determined to devote himself to sacred literature and to the reform of theology, and the Jerome project was an essential part of that larger program. He explains his intentions in several letters in late 1500 and early 1501.[8] What prompts him to emend and elucidate Jerome, he tells us, "is the goodness of the saintly man who of all Christians was by common consent the best scholar and best writer."[9] Today, inferior theologians hold sway, he declares, while Jerome "the supreme champion and expositor and ornament of our faith" is ill understood and sadly neglected. In a remarkable passage further extolling Jerome, he describes the difficult task he has taken upon himself:

> First of all, how difficult it will be to wipe away the errors which in the course of long ages have so profoundly penetrated the text. Secondly, look at the classical learning, the Greek scholarship, the histories to be found in him, and all those stylistic and rhetorical accomplishments in which he not only far outstrips all Christian writers, but even seems to rival Cicero himself. For my part at any rate, unless my affection for that saintly man is leading me astray, when I compare Jerome's prose with Cicero's, I seem to find something lacking in even the prince of prose writers. There is in our author such variety, such solidity of content, such fluency of argument, and while it is very difficult to demonstrate this kind of artistry in the works of good stylists, it is nevertheless extremely helpful. This is what I trust I may be able to do, provided the saint himself comes to my aid; and I hope that,

as a result, those who have hitherto admired Jerome for his reputation as a stylist may now admit that they never before understood the nature of his stylistic power.[10]

It was not until 1516 that that enterprise was completed. In September of that year Johann Froben published in Basel the great edition Erasmus had long ago envisaged. In the intervening years other projects, of course, had occupied Erasmus, and he authored some of his most famous and important books. He continued especially to work on Holy Scripture—preparing a commentary on Saint Paul, making a new Latin translation of the New Testament, editing the Greek text, and annotating it.[11] He wrote John Colet in 1504 that he was eager "to approach sacred scripture full sail, full gallop" and that he intended to spend all the rest of his life upon it.[12] He had earlier in 1504 discovered a manuscript of annotations by Lorenzo Valla collating and correcting the Vulgate text of the New Testament and subsequently published it.[13] It had considerable influence on him, but in these endeavors Jerome was his chief inspiration and guide. He knew that he followed in the saint's footsteps and continued his labors. Our two portraits come to mind. 1516, the year of the Jerome edition, also saw the culmination of Erasmus' work on Scripture. In March that year Froben published his Latin and Greek New Testament. The two great enterprises were complementary, and they had come to fruition together.

From 1511 to 1514 Erasmus was at Cambridge where he taught Greek and lectured on Jerome and where he resumed work on both his scriptural and Jerome projects.[14] He again took up the preparation of a revised edition of Jerome's letters, collating, emending, annotating. "I seem to myself inspired by some god," he declared, excited by his labors on Jerome's text. In May 1512 his Paris printer Josse Bade wrote him asking for the improved edition he was preparing.[15] Bade said that he had put about a rumor that he was expecting it, and he wanted to begin printing immediately. But Erasmus' copy was not yet ready for the press. By the time it was, he had changed printers and had joined forces with Froben in Basel.

The story of that transaction is an interesting one. A not too trustworthy bookseller and printer's agent, Franz Birckmann, diverted the manuscript of an expanded version of the *Adagia* and some other material which Erasmus had given him to deliver to Bade to the Basel firm instead.[16] Whether Erasmus connived or colluded in this diversion is moot, but it probably did not distress him. He was not entirely satisfied with the quality of Bade's work or with the adequacy of his Greek font, and a reprint of an early Aldine edition of the *Adagia* which the Basel firm had published in 1513, although it was pirated, he thought was handsomely done. It is very probable too that Erasmus knew that the Basel printer Johann Amerbach and his partner Johann Froben were preparing a complete edition of Saint Jerome and that this in particular drew him and his work to Basel. At any rate Erasmus left England in July 1514 and made his way to the bustling city on the great bend of the Rhine. There a very famous collaboration began. In the words of P. S. Allen, Erasmus' decision "brought together the greatest scholar and the greatest printer in Transalpine Europe."[17]

Amerbach had died the preceding December, but it had been his lifelong ambition to publish complete editions of the four Doctors of the Western Church. He had brought out an edition of Saint Ambrose in 1492 and of Saint Augustine in 1506 and had started work on a Jerome edition as early as 1507. "He had entertained the hope," his sons Bruno and Basil tell us, "that if the splendid theology of ancient times should come to life again that prickly and frigid kind of sophistical theology would have less influence and our Christians would be more generous and genuine."[18] It was a view that Erasmus wholeheartedly shared. Amerbach had gone to considerable effort and expense in gathering manuscripts of

Jerome and in collating and restoring his writings, and he had employed several notable scholars in this task, including Johann Reuchlin, Conrad Pellican, Gregor Reisch, the Carthusian prior at Freiburg, and Johann Kuno, a learned Dominican who has been called Erasmus' precursor in Basel.[19] He had also seen to the rigorous education of his sons Bruno, Basil, and Boniface so that they could assist in these endeavors. After their father's death they dutifully continued his undertaking together with Johann Froben. It was at this point that Erasmus entered the Basel scene, bringing his own work on the letters of Saint Jerome, as well as other important materials, with him. "If he had come to us at the right time," Amerbach's sons rather querulously declared, "he alone would have sufficed for every task."[20]

Erasmus' responsibility was the letters and other treatises of Jerome which went into the first four volumes of the edition, although he helped and advised on the project throughout. He was, so to speak, the editor-in-chief. He has given us several vivid accounts of his labors in emending and editing Jerome's text and of the character and importance of the great edition that was then in progress.[21] "I doubt if Jerome himself expended so much effort on the writing of his works as they will cost me in the correction," he declared. "At least I have thrown myself into this task so zealously that one could almost say that I have worked myself to death that Jerome might live again."[22] To Pope Leo X, to whom he had originally intended to dedicate the edition, he wrote that "in the noble German city of Basel the whole of Jerome is being born again," and he explained the reason for his efforts to give Jerome a new lease of life:

> I saw clearly that Saint Jerome is chief among the theologians of the Latin world, and is in fact almost the only writer we have who deserves the name of theologian . . . ; indeed he has such splendid gifts that Greece itself with all its learning can scarcely produce a man to be matched with him. What Roman eloquence, what mastery of the tongues, what a range

of knowledge in all antiquity and all history! And then his retentive memory, his happy knack of combining unexpected things, his perfect command of Holy Scripture! Above all, with his burning energy and the divine inspiration in that amazing heart, he can at the same moment delight us with his eloquence, instruct us with his learning, and sweep us away with his religious force. And yet the one man we possess who richly deserves to be read by all is the one author so much corrupted, so mixed with dirt and filth, that even scholars cannot understand him![23]

The work was finally finished in the summer of 1516, and the edition was on the market in late September. One of the great ambitions of Erasmus had been realized, one of his most significant enterprises had been accomplished.

The edition consisted of nine folio volumes and was the first *opera omnia* of the saint.[24] The first four volumes are letters, *apologiae*, and various treatises, the remaining five are scriptural commentaries and include (in volume 8) a trilingual psalter. Erasmus edited and annotated the first four, supplying them with prefaces, *argumenta* or summaries, and copious *scholia*. The Amerbach brothers apparently were in charge of the other five, the prefaces being in their name.[25] Erasmus dedicated the work to Archbishop William Warham of Canterbury, primate of England and lord chancellor of the realm, a devoted friend and patron, and wrote a long letter of dedication as a general preface to the edition.[26] He also composed a *Life* of Saint Jerome to serve as an introduction to his writings.[27] Both the dedicatory letter and the *Life* deserve careful attention.

Erasmus begins the letter of dedication by observing how the ancients treasured and preserved the works of outstanding authors but how in later time the writings of Christian authors, "men inspired by the Holy Spirit," have been allowed to perish or to be foully mutilated and corrupted. He blames the medieval schoolmen for this neglect and loss. They reduced literature to "a few sophistic niceties" and let the Fathers fall out of use so that Occam and other late scholastics would be read. The fate of Jerome especially has been monstrous. Even if no one else, he should have been preserved "complete and uncorrupted." This carries Erasmus into a ringing panegyric of the saint's incomparable gifts and qualities—his mental endowments, his brilliance of expression rivaling Cicero himself, his learning, his knowledge of languages, his mastery of Scripture, his lofty character and Christian life. He then expounds on his labors in restoring the battered text of Jerome. He is obsessive about the work and tedium and weariness involved: "I cannot think that Hercules consumed as much energy in taming a few monsters as I did in abolishing so many thousand blunders." But the effort, of course, was eminently worthwhile: "It is a river of gold, a well-stocked library, that a man acquires who possesses Jerome and nothing else." And in explaining to Archbishop Warham why he has dedicated the Jerome edition to him to whom he owes so much he also declares that the prelate perceives "that after the writings of the evangelists and apostles there is nothing more deserving of a Christian's attention."

This high praise of Jerome is continued in the *Life* of the saint that Erasmus wrote for the edition. It is the first critical biography of Jerome and one of Erasmus' most interesting compositions. As an extended historical work it stands alone among his writings, and it affords a prime example of the development of modern historical method within the context of Renaissance humanism. It is amazing that this work has not been better known or that it has not had a more prominent place in the Erasmian corpus.[28] Besides its historiographical values it reveals, as we might expect, in all its fullness Erasmus' understanding of Jerome and the central role the scholar-saint plays in his program of renewal and reform.

The historical authenticity of the *Life*—its *fides*—is the first quality that strikes the reader. In its opening pages Erasmus sets down the critical standards that will guide him in his narrative. He disavows the use of the "noble" or Platonic lie, the practice of telling fictitious tales for a good purpose, and affirms that he will give an honest account of Jerome's life. "I think nothing is better than to portray the saints just as they actually were," he writes, and he continues: "Truth has its own power matched by no artifice." He criticizes the medieval *Lives* of Jerome and declares that he has based his own *Life* on contemporary evidence and above all on the works of Jerome himself:

> For who would have a better knowledge of Jerome than Jerome himself? Or who would give a truer picture of him? . . . I therefore have looked into all Jerome's works and have reduced to narrative form the material I was able to gather from scattered parts of his writings. In doing this I invented nothing because to me the greatest miracle is the miracle of Jerome as he expresses himself to us in his many works of lasting and pre-eminent quality.[29]

What follows this incisive introduction is the chronological narrative of Jerome's life. It is not without shortcomings and obscurities, but is nevertheless an excellent biographical sketch, a work of serious scholarship and ample documentation, generally faithful to the principles Erasmus set down. Its focus is on the saint's education and studies, that is, on his preparation to be the great scholar, writer, and theologian he will become. Erasmus tells of his early training at home, his classical schooling in Rome, his concentration on rhetoric so that he might eventually enhance theology with "dignity of style." Then came travel and further study and finally Jerome's decision to follow a monastic life in the East. He took his library with him to Syria where his studies continued. He learned Holy Scripture word for word, and "as from the purest springs he drew the philosophy of Christ."[30] He read all the authors pagan and heretical, he despoiled the

Egyptians, he learned Hebrew and Chaldee. Finally he could take his place as a superb Christian scholar and theologian.

The import of all of this is obvious. Erasmus is asserting that this kind of training is essential for the theologian and is giving us Jerome as the model to imitate. He is also asserting that theology is the study of Holy Scripture and requires every talent, every skill, and he is defending this thesis against his scholastic opponents who had a very different concept of that sacred discipline. We are at the very heart of Erasmus' reform humanism: his aim to revitalize theological study, to restore the true theology—the *vera theologia*—of the early Church. In this endeavor Jerome led the way and represented the goal.

The third and last part of the *Life* takes up the defense of Jerome against his critics and continues this central theme. The chief of these critics are the *barbari*, the anti-humanist scholastic theologians who disapproved of Jerome's learning and denied him the status of a theologian. Erasmus derides them for taking the so-called dream of Jerome seriously[31] and attacks them for not recognizing in Jerome the hallmarks of a genuine theologian. "Who had a more thorough knowledge of the philosophy of Christ?", he asks. "Who expressed it more forcefully in his writings or in his life?"[32] The rhetorical questions Erasmus poses at this point constitute the climax of the *Life*. They define the theologian and elevate Jerome to that rank. They underscore the connection between Jerome and the New Testament which Erasmus had published earlier that year. They again remind us that Jerome's writings are the great companion piece of Scripture itself.

There is a second group of critics at the other end of the spectrum against whom Erasmus also defends Jerome. They are excessively humanistic and pedantically critical, and they include those who feel Jerome was not Ciceronian enough in his style. The charge is paradoxical in view of the story of the dream. Erasmus refutes their remarks, defends the saint's eloquence, and attacks the notion that the Christian author must speak exactly as Cicero did. "Cicero himself would have had to change his language if he were Jerome," he declares. His argument here foreshadows the longer attack he will make years later in his *Ciceronianus*. It is characteristic that Erasmus fights both extremes—those who exaggerated the demands of *bonae litterae* as well as those who ignored them entirely—in the name of effective humanist reform.

It was Erasmus' purpose in presenting Jerome and arguing his case that gave shape to the work and determined its specific character and thrust. The *Life* is a plea in behalf of the ideas and reforms Erasmus held most dear. Jerome thus appears as an ideal, an exemplar, a model to be followed. To tell his story and defend him against his critics was to argue the case for those reforms in theology and religious life Erasmus sought. Indeed, Erasmus identified with Jerome, and the *Life* is his own justification and defense. Eugene Rice has called it "a self-portrait."[33] Yet the validity of the *Life* is sound. Erasmus did break with the earlier hagiography of the saint and reconstructed his sketch on the basis of the historical evidence. His achievement was to draw so authentic an historical portrait within the context of his own reform program. His success in doing this is a measure not only of his own perception and skill but of the fundamental affinity between the two great scholars. Our two portraits again come to mind.

We say that Erasmus edited the letters of Saint Jerome. The term "letters" in this instance covers a wide variety of instructional, polemical, and exegetical writing that constitutes the most important segment of the Jerome corpus. Their restoring, editing, and annotating was the most difficult task of all, for although there were many earlier editions of these works the spurious and falsely ascribed were mixed with the genuine, and there were mutilations and interpolations throughout Jerome's text.[34] In this critical work, which required skilled judgment as well as erudition, Erasmus did an outstanding job, and his achievement has been hailed by modern scholars.[35] His method had its shortcomings, but, as Jacques Chomarat and others have pointed out, he was a pioneer and by the standards of his day what he achieved was remarkable.[36] He did restore the authentic Jerome. He identified the spurious works and assembled and arranged most of them in a separate volume (volume 2 in the 1516 edition, volume 4 in the later ones). He wrote extensive *censurae*, commenting on their authorship, and two lengthy prefaces (in volume 2), discussing the problem of false attributions, bemoaning the worthless *spuria* ascribed to Jerome, and berating the "impostor" who dared fabricate such drivel. His forte as an editor, as well as what would seem to be his main preoccupation as such, was in that field. The Amerbach brothers hailed him on that score as "a man of the surest discernment."[37] In his first preface in volume 2 he explains how this ability to discern is based essentially on recognizing the author's style. "The surest sign and truly the Lydian stone [in identifying an author]," he writes, "is the character and quality of his speech. As each individual has his own appearance, his voice, his own character and disposition, so each has his own style of writing. And the quality of mind is manifest in speech even more than the likeness of the body is reflected in a mirror."[38] The axiom *Le style est l'homme-même* had no more ardent disciple than Erasmus.

Another important feature of Erasmus' edition is the annotations or *scholia* that accompany the text throughout. These are his commentaries, and they "still remain," according to Denys Gorce, "an unequaled mine for the scholar and commentator on Jerome."[39] They are appended to all the letters, and they contain a great variety of information and comment. Most are in the nature of footnotes, though there are some more extended *antidoti*, and for the first letter in the edition—the letter to Heliodorus on the solitary life[40]—there is a comprehensive rhetorical analysis. Jacques Chomarat in his *Grammaire et rhétorique chez Erasme* has discussed this latter commentary at some length using it as an example to bear out his basic theme that Erasmus sought above all to unite eloquence and piety.[41] In this endeavor Jerome was his model; Quintilian and the New Testament, his "double inspiration." The *scholia* were intended to elucidate Jerome and help one read him more intelligently, more appreciatively. They explain terms and figures of speech, they identify names and places, they indicate scriptural and literary allusions, they clarify obscurities, they give variants and discuss corrections in the text. Quite often, and particularly in the *antidoti*, they contain characteristically Erasmian remarks on the ways and practices of Christians in his own time which underline the contrast with the example or ideal in the early Church. These pointed criticisms, like those elsewhere in Erasmus' writings, were a source of irritation and complaint among his critics and were responsible at least in part for the re-editing of Jerome's works under Catholic auspices in the latter half of the century.[42]

Here are a few samples of these more pungent comments taken somewhat randomly from volume I of the edition. In a *scholium* appended to the second letter of his edition—Jerome's letter to Nepotian on the life of clerics and priests[43]—Erasmus writes: "It should be noted in this passage that clerics had once been prohibited by imperial laws from inheriting property. Finally, since Saint Jerome throughout this letter wants priests to be poor in material goods but rich in learning and piety he does not fully agree with the general conviction of our day which holds that the Church is especially strengthened and adorned by these riches."[44] An *antidotus* also appended to the letter further develops this theme.[45] Erasmus cautions against interpreting Jerome too literally when he appears to demand complete poverty of the clergy. The saint, he tells us, is overstating his case and is reacting against an increasing worldliness among the clergy. The lesson for us is to examine our ways and amend our lives. "Our lives should be such," he writes, "that we would no longer have to distort the teachings of Christ to conform with our behavior and with the traditions of men." In another *antidotus*—one attached to Jerome's letter of advice to the young monk Rusticus[46]—Erasmus points up the difference between the freer and less structured religious life in Jerome's day and the highly formalized monastic life in his own.[47] He speculates that it may be better for the Church today if there were fewer monasteries and far fewer rules and ceremonials. The latter, he says in a parting shot, "can make one superstitious but not devout." A *scholium* attached to one of Jerome's entries in his *Catalogue of Ecclesiastical Writers* contains another typical Erasmian observation. He is referring back to an argument in the text about the exact day of the Passover. "We dispute fiercely about trifles of this sort," Erasmus writes," . . . but about the most insane wars which for so many years now embroil everything sacred and profane the theologians are silent, the preachers say nothing."[48] Even in the index of Jerome's works which Erasmus prepared as a part of his introductory material we find surprisingly a sharp censorious remark embedded in a listing of lost works of Jerome. He says: "[Jerome] translated Holy Scripture for men of his own language, that is, he turned it into Dalmatian. Yet today it is thought a sin if Scripture is read in the vernacular."[49] Erasmus lost few opportunities to drive home a point, to express himself sharply, succinctly, suddenly on controversial issues that were of the utmost importance to him. He raised hackles and made enemies thereby, but his annotations and comments greatly enriched his edition and added to its relevance and impact as a work of humanist reform.

III

We have been emphasizing that Erasmus was a reformer and that his scholarly and literary work was an integral and fundamental part of his reform program. His aim was to reform theology by returning it to its scriptural and patristic sources. This meant replacing the theology of the schools—the "modern" theology of the Occamists, Scotists, and other dialecticians—with what Erasmus deemed the genuine theology of the early Church: the *vetus ac vera theologia*. Everything else would flow from that—the restoration of religion, the reform of the individual Christian, the amelioration of Christian society. In this return to the sources Holy Scripture came first, of course, especially the Gospels and Epistles, but after this "literature of Christ" came the early Fathers. Their authority derived from their closeness in time as well as in spirit to the divine source, and their chief value lay in interpreting the sacred text and moving us to a fuller understanding and acceptance of it. They instructed and inspired us in living a Christian life, for theology was essentially practical in Erasmus' view, a guide to life rather than a subject for debate, a matter of transformation rather than speculation.

Nearly all of Erasmus' career and work can be seen in this light—from his first meeting with Colet at Oxford in 1499 to his posthumous edition of Origen in 1536. He had been deeply impressed by Colet's exegetical approach in his lectures on Saint Paul's Epistles, and he applauded his doing battle with "the squalid mob of carping theologues . . . for the sake of restoring to as much of its early splendour and dignity as you can that ancient true theology."[50] Colet wanted Erasmus to join him in this endeavor, but conscious of his present inadequacy Erasmus declined the invitation. He declared, however, that "as soon as I feel myself to possess the necessary stamina and strength, I shall come personally to join your party, and will give devoted, if not distinguished, service to the defence of theology."[51] Prophetic words indeed! Erasmus did join Colet's party and gave distinguished as well as devoted service to the common cause. Returning to the continent in 1500, he set about mastering Greek, and he began to envisage the edition of Jerome that finally came to fruition in 1516.

Why did Jerome occupy a place of such prime importance in Erasmus' reform plans? There is hardly any mystery about it. As Erasmus tells us over and over again, he believes Jerome is the greatest of the Latin Fathers and that even Greece could scarcely match him. The saint's erudition, his love of letters, his knowledge of languages, his superb style elevated him above all the others. He was the model of what the theologian ought to be—the "prince of theologians"—and his restoration therefore was synonymous with the restoration of theology itself. We can, of course, dig deeper into the reasons why Erasmus had so marked a predilection for Jerome. A good part of it, I believe, is already revealed in that early letter of Erasmus' we quoted at the outset, the letter he wrote as a young canon at Steyn saying he had read and copied all of Jerome's letters.[52] He admired their literary quality, their elegance of style. They were decisive proof that there need not be a divorce between religion and culture. Jerome in fact embodied their union and could serve therefore as an exemplar for the young canon already captivated by that revival of classical letters which is the very essence of Renaissance humanism. The saint's literary excellence, his eloquence, his "stylistic power" that rivals Cicero's, Erasmus tells us, and in some respects even surpasses it also pointed the way to that renewal of theology which soon became Erasmus' primary goal. As we mentioned above, referring to Jacques Chomarat's *Grammaire et rhétorique chez Erasme*, Erasmus sought above all to unite eloquence and piety, to forge what has been called, in the best sense, a "rhetorical theology." Here Jerome was the model and ideal.

Intimately connected with Jerome's literary excellence and his eloquence was his classical learning. This in turn presupposed his knowledge of Greek, an accomplishment that gave him in Erasmus' estimation a distinct advantage over Saint Augustine. His formidable erudition along with his stylistic skill commended him naturally to the humanist, but more important was the bearing of this on his work as a theologian and its contribution to his scriptural studies. His training in rhetoric enabled him to endow theology with "dignity of style." His classical learning gave rich cultural context to his writing. His knowledge of languages, which included not only Latin and Greek but also Hebrew and Chaldee, made it possible for him to work with all the original texts of Holy Scripture. "What Roman eloquence, what mastery of the tongues, what a range of knowledge in all antiquity and all history!" as Erasmus exclaimed in his letter to Pope Leo X.[53] This "mastery of the tongues" certainly was one of the most important attractions of Jerome for Erasmus. The return to the sources and the careful study of the ancient texts in their original languages are the distinguishing marks of the humanist scholar. That Jerome did this so extensively and so notably with Holy Scripture gave Erasmus a precedent and justification for his own work on the New Testament and established perhaps the closest bond between them. Once again our two portraits come to mind. The approach and method involved in this study of Scripture and in its exegesis has been called grammatical or philological, the emphasis being on the language of the sacred text and on the use and meaning of its words in their original context. As a theological method it stood in sharp contrast to the scholastic and was a subject of great controversy between Erasmus and his critics, but it joined him with Jerome in a single endeavor.[54] If the prince of humanists sought to replace scholasticism with a "rhetorical theology," he strove also for one that would be basically and thoroughly "grammatical" as well.[55]

Erasmus' singular preference for Jerome has often been contrasted with his attitude toward Saint Augustine, the other early Father whose influence was so pervasive and whose fame throughout the Middle Ages was so high. In his *Life* of Jerome Erasmus in discussing the correspondence that took place between the two saints remarked that Augustine was superior to Jerome only in his episcopal dignity and that he was inferior in all other respects (a sentence, by the way, he omitted when he revised his edition of the letters in 1524).[56] He also took issue in the *Life* with the Italian humanist Francesco Filelfo who had once said that Augustine was superior in dialectics but that Jerome surpassed him in eloquence. "It is not my purpose to diminish in any way the attainments of Augustine," Erasmus wrote, "but the facts themselves proclaim that Jerome surpassed Augustine in dialectics no less than he outstripped him in eloquence and that he was no less Augustine's superior in learning than he was in excellence of style."[57] Johann Eck, Luther's famous opponent, in a letter to Erasmus a few years later declared that he agreed with the judgment of Filelfo and bemoaned the fact that Erasmus was critical of Augustine and had disparaged him in one of his New Testament annotations.[58] He accused Erasmus of having failed to read Augustine. Erasmus replied at length defending his preference for Jerome.[59] He ridiculed the notion that he had not read Augustine. He "was the author I read first of them all," he declared, " . . . and the more I read him, the more I feel satisfied with my estimate of the two of them." He urged Eck "to read Jerome with more attention, and you will vote for my side." He then launched into a comparison of Jerome with Augustine, rehearsing Jerome's advantages at every point of the way—in birthplace, education, early Christian upbringing, long years devoted to the study of Holy Scripture. And he especially stressed that Jerome knew Greek. "All philosophy and all theology in those days belonged to the Greeks," Erasmus declared, yet "Augustine knew no Greek." This deficiency obviously was of decisive importance for the great humanist.

I might note parenthetically that Luther, somewhat paradoxically, shared the view of his arch-opponent Johann Eck concerning the superiority of Saint Augustine and disagreed sharply with Erasmus on this matter.[60] His reasons however were different from Eck's and dogmatically rooted. But that is another story and quite beyond the scope of the subject we have been discussing.

IV

My topic has been the bond between Erasmus and Saint Jerome and its significance. I have dealt extensively with the first part of that topic. Let me say in conclusion a few words at least about the second part. What is the significance of it all? For Erasmus, of course, the bond was of the utmost importance. From the outset Jerome was a major influence on him—an inspiration, a model, an ideal. I am told by a noted classical scholar that Erasmus' own literary style most closely resembles Saint Jerome's. Certainly his humanism does,[61] and so do his scriptural focus and approach and achievement. And the precedent of Jerome was assurance and justification for Erasmus in his own endeavors. We can point also to a broader significance. The affinity between the two great scholars is a classic example of that revival of antiquity—that return to the sources—we associate so basically with the Renaissance. The bond is a witness of a "discovery" but also of an assimilation, and this in turn generated intellectual ferment and religious reform. It is part of a larger picture, to be sure, but it is a very characteristic, integral, and important part. And finally, I think, it reveals the variety and richness of the Christian tradition and serves to remind us of its historic potential for personal and cultural renewal.

Notes

1. Eugene F. Rice, Jr., *Saint Jerome in the Renaissance* (Baltimore, 1985), pp. 104–107. On the Fabriano portrait see Federico Zeri, *Italian Paintings in the Walters Art Gallery* I (Baltimore, 1976), pp. 189–91 and plate 94.

2. "The Mystery of the Metsys Portrait," *Erasmus in English*, 7 (1975), 18–21; and Lorne Campbell et al., "Quentin Metsys, Desiderius Erasmus, Pieter Gillis and Thomas More," *The Burlington Magazine*, 120 (November 1978), 716–24.

3. Rice, *Saint Jerome in the Renaissance*; John M. McManamon, s.j., "Pier Paolo Vergerio (the Elder) and the Beginnings of the Humanist Cult of Jerome," *The Catholic Historical Review*, 71 (1985), 353–71; and Millard Meiss, "Scholarship and Penitence in the Early Renaissance: The Image of St. Jerome," *The Painter's Choice: Problems in the Interpretation of Renaissance Art* (New York, 1976), pp. 189–202.

4. Allen II, p. 210.

5. CWE 1, Letter 22.

6. That is, *The Antibarbarians*, in CWE 23.

7. CWE 1, Letter 23. His correspondence with Cornelis Gerard at this time gives us a superb picture of Erasmus' humanist beginnings.

8. CWE 1, Letters 138, 139, 141; CWE 2, Letter 149.

9. CWE 1, Letter 141.

10. CWE 1, Letter 141, lines 41–55.

11. CWE 3, Letter 373, introduction; Letter 384, introduction; and Jerry Bentley, *Humanists and Holy Writ* (Princeton, 1983), chap. 4, pp. 112–93.

12. CWE 2, Letter 181.

13. CWE 2, Letter 182.

14. *Erasmus and Cambridge: The Cambridge Letters of Erasmus*, trans. D. F. S. Thomson (Toronto, 1963), pp. 39–43; and CWE 2, Letters 245, 248, 264, 270, 273, 281, 296.

15. CWE 2, Letter 263.

16. Erasmus tells the story in a letter of December 2, 1513, in CWE 2, Letter 283, lines 181–96.

17. *Erasmus: Lectures and Wayfaring Sketches* (Oxford, 1934), p. 124. Erasmus describes his trip to Basel and his first meeting with Johann Froben in a long letter to Jacob Wimpfeling, September 21, 1514, in CWE 3, Letter 305.

18. HO, V, title[v]. See CWE 61, p. 234. I have used the copy of the HO in the library of St. Joseph's Seminary in Yonkers, New York. The nine volumes are bound in five, and the prefatory material precedes the foliation in volume I.

19. HO, V, title^v. Beatus Rhenanus in his *Life* of Erasmus gives a similar account; see CHR³, pp. 55–56. See also *Die Amerbach Korrespondenz* I, ed. Alfred Hartmann, 5 vols. (Basel, 1942–1958), and H. D. Saffrey, "Un humaniste dominicain, Jean Cuno de Nuremberg, précurseur d'Erasme à Bâle," *Bibliothèque d'humanisme et renaissance*, 33 (1971), 19–62.

20. HO, V, title^v.

21. CWE 3, Letters 333, lines 67–105; 334, lines 104–70; 335, lines 229–362; and 396, the dedicatory preface to HO. Letters 333, 334, and 335 (together with 337, Erasmus' famous reply to Martin Dorp) were the first of Erasmus' letters to be published by Froben in August 1515. *Adage* III.i.1 ("The Labors of Hercules") also contains an account of his Jerome labors.

22. CWE 3, Letter 333, lines 85–88.

23. CWE 3, Letter 335, lines 232–47.

24. See note 18. Other copies of the 1516 edition are in the Folger Shakespeare Library, the Beinecke Library at Yale University, and the Newberry Library in Chicago. A second revised edition was published by Froben in 1524–1526 and was reprinted by Sebastian Gryphius in Lyons in 1530. Claude Chevallon published a third revised edition in Paris in 1533–1534. The Froben firm brought out further editions in 1536–1537, 1553, and 1565. The most substantial study of the edition is Denys Gorce, "La patristique dans la réforme d'Erasme," *Festgabe Joseph Lortz*, 2 vols. (Baden-Baden, 1958), I, 233–76. Rice, *Saint Jerome in the Renaissance*, chap. 5, also gives an extensive analysis.

25. See Allen II, p. 211. Allen questions the ascription of the prefaces to the Amerbachs, though the personal references in HO, V, title^v, would seem to warrant the attribution.

26. CWE 3, Letter 396.

27. The composite text is HV, pp. 134–90. On the *Life* see Joseph Coppens, "Le portrait de saint Jérôme d'après Erasme," *Colloquia Erasmiana Turonensia*, ed. J.-C. Margolin, 2 vols. (Toronto, 1972), II, 821–28; J. B. Maguire, "Erasmus' Biographical Masterpiece: *Hieronymi Stridonensis Vita*," *Renaissance Quarterly*, 26 (1973), 265–73; and John C. Olin, "*Eloquentia, Eruditio, Fides*: Erasmus' *Life of Jerome*," *Acta Conventus Neo-Latini Sanctandreani*, ed. I. D. McFarlane (Binghamton, N.Y., 1986), pp. 269–74. The English translation of the *Life* is in CWE 61, pp. 15–62.

28. It was published, of course, in the early Erasmus editions of Jerome, and it was printed separately in 1517 and 1519. It was not included, however, in the Leiden *Opera omnia* of Erasmus, 10 vols. (1703–1706); nor are there any other editions of it aside from Ferguson's composite text in HV and the English translation in CWE 61.

29. HV, lines 125–33. All translations from the *Life* are by James F. Brady and John C. Olin.

30. HV, lines 492–93. Erasmus first used the term "the philosophy of Christ" in the *Paraclesis* or introduction to his New Testament of 1516. His use of it in the *Life* of Jerome links the two editions.

31. Jerome's story of the "dream" is in his *Ep.* 22.30. Years later in his polemic with Rufinus he minimized its importance.

32. HV, lines 1212–14.

33. Rice, *Saint Jerome in the Renaissance*, p. 132.

34. See ibid., pp. 120ff., and the preface to Jerome's *opera* in Migne, *Patrologia latina* 22.xi–xiv. There were more than twenty printed editions of Jerome's letters prior to Erasmus'. He used two of the earliest ones: Sweynheym and Pannartz' Roman *editio princeps* of 1468 and Peter Schoeffer's Mainz edition of 1470. Very little is known about his manuscript sources. The Amerbach brothers tell us that their father procured copies of Jerome's works from "innumerable libraries" and again that "nearly all the libraries of Germany supplied copies." HO, V, title^v.

35. Gorce, "La patristique dans la réforme d'Erasme," pp. 272–76; Rice, *Saint Jerome in the Renaissance*, p. 120; Pierre Petitmengin, "Comment étudier l'activité d'Erasme, éditeur de textes antiques?" *Colloquia Erasmiana Turonensia*, I, 217–22; E. J. Kinney, *The Classical Text* (Berkeley, 1974), pp. 50–51; and *Saint Jérôme: Lettres*, ed. and trans. Jérôme Labourt, 8 vols. (Paris, 1949–1964), I, li.

36. Jacques Chomarat, *Grammaire et rhétorique chez Erasme*, 2 vols. (Paris, 1982), pp. 497–98.

37. HO, V, title^v.

38. HO, II, fol. 3^v. See CWE 61, p. 76.

39. "La patristique dans la réforme d'Erasme," p. 273.

40. *Ep.* 14.

41. Pp. 536–40.

42. The Catholic replacement for Erasmus' edition was the revision by Mariano Vittori published in Rome by Paulus Manutius

in nine volumes in 1565–1574. See Rice, *Saint Jerome in the Renaissance*, pp. 154–56. The first Jesuit author, Peter Canisius, also edited and published a single volume of selected letters of Jerome, to which he added a preface, dated 1565, taking sharp issue with Erasmus' *scholia*. He wished that Erasmus had confined himself to editing the letters without injecting his "poisonous" remarks.

43. *Ep.* 52.
44. HO, I, fol. 5^v.
45. HO, I, fols. 6^{r-v}. A very similar *antidotus* in appended to the preceding letter.
46. *Ep.* 125. The letter is number 4 in Erasmus' edition.
47. HO, I, fol. 20.
48. HO, I, 140. I noted the passage was scratched out in the copy in Yale's Beinecke Library.
49. HO, I, sig. gamma 6. See Craig R. Thompson, "Jerome and the Testimony of Erasmus in Disputes over the Vernacular Bible," *Proceedings of the PMR Conference*, 6 (1981), 1–36.
50. CWE 1, Letter 108, lines 22ff.
51. CWE 1, Letter 108, lines 122–27.
52. CWE 1, Letter 22.
53. CWE 3, Letter 335, lines 239–40.
54. August Humbert, *Les origines de la théologie moderne. I. La Renaissance de l'antiquité chrétienne* (Paris, 1911), pp. 228–38. Humbert emphasizes their kinship on this score.
55. Both Chomarat, *Grammaire et rhétorique chez Erasme*, and André Godin, *Érasme: Lecteur d'Origène* (Geneva, 1982), stress this double aim of Erasmus'.
56. HV, lines 905–907.
57. HV, lines 1256–61.
58. CWE 5, Letter 769, lines 97–114. Eck does not refer to Erasmus' critique of Filelfo in the *Life* of Jerome.
59. CWE 6, Letter 844, lines 132–288.
60. Rice, *Saint Jerome in the Renaissance*, pp. 138–39.
61. See Edwin A. Quain, s.j., "St. Jerome as a Humanist," in *A Monument to St. Jerome*, ed. F. X. Murphy (New York, 1952), pp. 201–32.

2
Erasmus and His Edition of Saint Hilary

UNTIL QUITE RECENTLY the interest of Renaissance humanists in the writings of the early Church Fathers has been sadly neglected. The most glaring example of this disregard perhaps is in the case of Erasmus. This "prince of humanists" certainly has been widely and deeply studied, yet his patristic scholarship—which has been called "the core of his intellectual life" and to which it has been said that he devoted "the better part of his existence"[1]—has been ignored generally. For example, in his biography of Erasmus Preserved Smith dismissed this enormous segment of his life's work in a few pages in a chapter dealing with Erasmus' "miscellaneous writings," and J. E. Sandys, in his three-volume *History of Classical Scholarship*, gave but a sentence to it.[2] The why of this neglect is hard to understand, but the fact remains. The situation is happily being remedied, however, and thanks to the efforts of many scholars we are gaining a better understanding and appreciation of the religious aspect of Renaissance humanism and of the biblical and patristic scholarship it embraced.[3]

It was my intention originally to deal with Erasmus and the Latin Fathers, but I soon became aware that the subject is too vast. The words of Werner Jaeger can be quoted as an indication of its breadth and importance: "In the last analysis, his Christian humanism goes back to the Greek Fathers who had created it in the fourth century. But his direct authorities were in the main the Latin Fathers, many of whose works he edited, along with the New Testament. St. Augustine's name comes to mind first of all in this connection."[4] Since space does not permit me to explore adequately this entire theme, I shall content myself with a more limited approach. I shall center my remarks on only one of Erasmus' patristic editions, but an edition particularly interesting for its dedication and preface and for the example it affords of how Erasmus in the context of the religious crisis in the sixteenth century drew on the patristic heritage for guidance and support. I refer to his edition of the works of Saint Hilary of Poitiers which appeared in 1523.

Erasmus' edition of Hilary was the fourth large patristic edition that he published, following his monumental edition of Saint Jerome in 1516, an edition of Saint Cyprian in 1520, and an edition of Arnobius the Younger's commentaries on the Psalms in 1522. He had begun also to work on an edition of Saint Augustine, but that task was very formidable and only *The City of God* which he had persuaded Vives to edit had appeared. (The complete Augustine was published in 1529 in ten folio volumes.) His purpose in all this editorial work was the reform of theology through a return to its scriptural and patristic sources, and he viewed the Fathers, whom he termed the ancient theologians, as the surest guides to Holy Scripture and the Christian life. They combined learning and piety in the most meaningful expression of the faith and stood in sharp contrast to the barren and disputatious theologians of his own day. His goal in brief was to replace the prevailing theology of the schools with the genuine theology of the early Church—the *vetus ac vera theologia*. Therein he believed lay the key to renewal and reform in every other sphere. It was a perspective and a purpose characteristic of the humanism of that age, and Erasmus was viewed as its chief representative, "the first author in our times of the rebirth of theology," to quote one of his many admirers.[5]

Like all his other patristic editions, the edition of Hilary was first published by the Froben press in Basel. After late

1521 Erasmus resided permanently in that bustling city, and he worked very closely with the great master printer Johann Froben. His Hilary, which came off the press in February 1523, was a large folio of more than 800 pages and was an *opera omnia* of the fourth-century Father. It was essentially a revised and improved edition of the works of Saint Hilary which had been edited by Robert Fortuné and published by Josse Bade in Paris in 1511.[6] Erasmus has emended the text, especially of Hilary's major work, *De trinitate*, and has indicated numerous variant readings in the margins. He collated the Paris edition with certain manuscripts available to him, of only one of which do we have any record—a manuscript sent by a friend, Maternus Hatten of Speyer, in early 1522.[7] It is a more handsome volume than the earlier edition, and it contains a long and extremely interesting preface by Erasmus in the form of a dedicatory letter.

The work was dedicated to Jean de Carondelet, a high official at the Hapsburg court in the Low Countries. Carondelet belonged to a prominent Burgundian family whose members had long served the Hapsburgs. His father had been chancellor of Burgundy under the Emperor Maximilian. He himself had been a secretary to the young Prince Charles and had accompanied him to Spain in 1517. Shortly afterward he was appointed archbishop of Palermo, although he never took up residence in that far-off see. At the time of the dedication he was chief counselor to Charles's regent in the Low Countries, his aunt Margaret of Austria, and he was unquestionably one of the most important personages at the Hapsburg court. Erasmus counted him among his friends and patrons. At this time Erasmus was deeply concerned about the influence of his critics, particularly at Louvain, who were connecting him with Luther and blaming him for the dissidence and heresy that had become so widespread, and he sought the understanding and support of important people. The dedication to Carondelet clearly fits into that pattern, and the edition itself—and indeed the example of Hilary confronting the Arian heretics of the fourth century—afforded an excellent opportunity for Erasmus to defend his own point of view and to clarify and substantiate his own position in the Lutheran controversy. The preface of the work amply bears this out.[8]

Erasmus opens his preface with a discussion of the corrupt state of the manuscripts of Hilary's texts and of the rashness of scribes who have taken great liberties with what he wrote.[9] They have excised, they have added, they have mutilated—and Erasmus gives us several examples of this tampering with the text. Having thus unburdened himself, he proceeds to discuss Hilary's works, beginning with his masterwork, the *De trinitate,* which the saint wrote to affirm and prove the divine nature of Christ against the doctrine of the Arians.[10] This almost immediately became the springboard for some very pointed observations and the development of a characteristic Erasmian theme. He pictures Hilary as silent at first in the face of Arianism, reluctant to become involved in such widespread dissension, and deploring the necessity of probing into and pronouncing on matters far beyond our understanding.[11] The parallel with Erasmus' own attitude is obvious. He reasons that the ancients may be pardoned because the early heretics forced them to make doctrinal statements, but asks what excuse we have for our excessive theologizing. And what tumult, what discord results from it! "The sum and substance of our religion is peace and concord," he declares in a famous sentence from the preface. "This can hardly remain the case unless we define as few matters as possible and leave each individual's judgment free on many questions."[12] Erasmus then assails the scholastic theologians for their inordinate defining and their contentiousness, and he lays it down that the mark of true theology is "to define nothing beyond what is recorded in Holy Scripture, but to dispense in good faith what is recorded there."[13]

This pungent message having been delivered, Erasmus returns to the subject of Hilary's *De trinitate* and comments on his style, his borrowing from the Greeks, his "imitation" of Quintilian, and similar matters, after which he takes up a second work of Hilary's, the *De synodis*. This leads him into a brief but important excursion sparked by what he considered Hilary's caution in making dogmatic assertions. I should like to quote the memorable passage that now follows:

> Once faith was more of a way of life than of a profession of articles. Soon necessity inspired the imposition of articles, but these were few and apostolic in their moderation. Then the wickedness of the heretics made for a more precise examination of the sacred books, and intransigence necessitated the definition of certain matters by the authority of synods. Finally faith began to reside in the written word rather than in the soul, and there were almost as many faiths as men. Articles increased, but sincerity decreased: contention boiled over, charity grew cold. The teachings of Christ which in former times were not touched by the clash of words began to depend on the support of philosophy: this was the first step of the Church on the downward path. There was an increase in wealth and an accretion of power. Furthermore, the intervention of imperial authority in this situation did not much improve the purity of faith. At length the consequence of all this was sophistical controversy and the eruption of thousands of articles. And then it became a matter of intimidation and threats. Although life may abandon us, although faith may be more on our lips than in our hearts, although that genuine understanding of Holy Scripture may fail us, yet we force men by intimidation to believe what they do not believe, to love that they do not love, and to understand what they do not understand. Compulsion is incompatible with sincerity, and nothing is pleasing to Christ unless it is voluntary.[14]

I scarcely recall any other passage in Erasmus so pithy and full of substance and expressive of his basic views. He seems to have condensed nearly all his leading ideas into a solid mass—a large cannonball, so to speak, to hurl at his scholastic critics. There are many familiar elements in this passage, but two especially stand out: one, the view that the decline and loss of faith is related to the formulation of articles and the development of a more elaborate theology; two, the notion that force must not be used to compel men "to believe what they do not believe." This last sentiment, far in advance of its time, is most interesting to consider in view of the situation and the practice that prevailed then and in view of the person Erasmus is addressing. Carondelet was delighted with the dedication, but one wonders how he read these particular remarks.[15]

Erasmus continues again, speaking of Hilary's works, though he very soon goes off into another digression, a long and somewhat rambling one but one well supplied with pertinent lessons and observations drawn from the example of Saint Hilary. He notes that Hilary in his writings against the Arians rarely has anything to say about the Holy Spirit, and he gives the reason either that he was concerned mainly with the question of the divinity of the Son or that like all the ancients he did not dare to go beyond what was set down in Holy Scripture—and nowhere there, says Erasmus, is the Holy Spirit explicitly called God.[16] He compares this restraint and reverence on the part of the ancients with the brashness of theologians today. "Indeed the progress of the Church," he claims, "at first depended on purity of life rather than on an exact knowledge of the divine nature, and it has never sustained a greater loss than when it seemed to make the greatest possible advances in philosophical knowledge."[17] Not that learning is evil in itself, but that it often begets factions and dissension. And personal feelings become involved in our controversies, and we are carried away, and responding to one error we fall into another. Erasmus gives some instances of this among the ancients including Hilary who lashes out in anger at the Arians and who sometimes seems not to take into sufficient account the human nature of Christ.[18] There is warning here for the bishops and theologians of our day, Erasmus feels, and he proceeds to show

how one must have self-control and moderation in dealing with heresy.

This part of the preface is especially relevant to the Lutheran quarrel which had by then assumed such serious proportions. Erasmus lambastes those who, defending papal authority, exaggerate it extravagantly and are unbridled in their attacks on others. When the dispute becomes violent on both sides, the truth is lost on both sides, he declares in a maxim that serves to justify that middle road he sought to follow.[19] Therefore he urges fairness and restraint, and he concludes: "Let us always keep before our eyes the gentleness of Him who, although He alone was free from all error, nevertheless did not extinguish the smoking flax, nor crush the bruised reed."[20] This model with its reference to the prophecy of Isaiah which Saint Matthew quoted is one that Erasmus will frequently offer at this time when speaking about Luther and how he should be handled.

After this, Erasmus reverts to the works of Hilary and enters into an extended discussion of his knowledge of Hebrew and Greek and specifically of his translation and explanation of a particular phrase in one of the Psalms. The discussion ends by acknowledging that although Hilary's Greek was faulty it was put to good use—a perception that allows Erasmus to take a parting shot at his critics. Where are those, he asks, who say that Greek literature is of no value. "Where are those individuals—camels rather than men—who bleat that nothing comes out of Greek literature except heresies?"[21] The appelation "camel" refers explicitly to the Louvain Carmelite Nicolaas Baechem ('Egmondanus'), an arch-opponent of Erasmus' and one attacking him fiercely at this time. Erasmus is punning with the designation "Carmelite."[22]

He now brings his preface to a close. He asks that Carondelet accept the dedication so that the luster of his name may win favor for Hilary among students of theology. Some are disdainful of the ancient authors and ungrateful to those to whom we owe so much, he writes. What could we accomplish in scriptural studies without their help? Not that St. Thomas and Duns Scotus should be entirely rejected, but that our regard for them should not lead us to "clamour against good literature happily springing up again everywhere." Reverence is due the ancient authors and fairness the modern ones, and "let furious contention, the bane of peace and concord, be absent everywhere."[23]

Thus he ends his appeal to Carondelet and the statement and defense of his own point of view at this critical time. His comments and themes are his own, but it is remarkable—one might say ingenious—how he employed this occasion to present them anew and how he drew on Hilary and used his example to underscore and support them. However, Erasmus' prescriptions and advice had little effect, and the preface unfortunately became one of his most controversial writings. Propositions from it were censured by the Sorbonne in 1526 and bitterly attacked at the Valladolid conference in Spain in 1527.[24] The letter is nevertheless a striking instance of the way Erasmus understood and made use of the patristic heritage, and the edition remains one of the many achievements of his humanist scholarship and his reform purpose.

Notes

1. The quotations are from E. F. Rice, "The Humanist Idea of Christian Antiquity and the Impact of Greek Patristic Work on Sixteenth-Century Thought," in *Classical Influences on European Culture, A.D. 1500–1700*, ed. R. R. Bolgar (Cambridge, 1976), p. 200, and Henri de Lubac, *Exégèse médiévale* II (Paris, 1964), p. 431, respectively.

2. Preserved Smith, *Erasmus: A Study of His Life, Ideals, and Place in History* (New York, 1923), pp. 189–93, and J. E. Sandys,

A History of Classical Scholarship II (Cambridge, 1908), pp. 130–31. R. R. Bolgar in his introduction to *Classical Influences on European Culture*, p. 18, has called attention to Sandys' scanty reference.

3. I am thinking particularly of the following: Charles Trinkaus, *In Our Image and Likeness: Humanity and Divinity in Italian Humanist Thought*, 2 vols. (Chicago, 1970); E. F. Rice, Jr., "The Humanist Idea of Christian Antiquity: Lefèvre d'Étaples and His Circle," *Studies in the Renaissance*, 9 (1962) 126–60; Hanna H. Gray, "Valla's *Encomium* of St. Thomas Aquinas and the Humanist Conception of Christian Antiquity," in *Essays in History and Literature: Presented by Fellows of The Newberry Library to Stanley Pargellis*, ed. Heinz Bluhm (Chicago, 1965), pp. 35–71; and Charles L. Stinger, *Humanism and the Church Fathers: Ambrogio Traversari (1386–1439) and Christian Antiquity in the Italian Renaissance* (Albany, N.Y., 1977). WERNER JAEGER IN THE CONCLUDING PAGES OF HIS *Early Christianity and Greek Paideia* (Cambridge, Mass., 1961) also stresses the importance of patristic influence on Renaissance and Erasmian humanism.

4. Jaeger, *Early Christianity and Greek Paideia*. The most extensive study of patristic influence on Erasmus is Charles Béné, *Erasme et saint Augustin, ou Influence de saint Augustin sur l'humanisme d'Erasme* (Geneva, 1969) where, as the title indicates, the paramount influence of Augustine is stressed. Another study in this area, focusing chiefly on Erasmus' edition of St. Jerome, is Denys Gorce's "La patristique dans la réforme d'Erasme," in *Festgabe Joseph Lortz*, 2 vols. (Baden-Baden, 1958), I, 233–76. See chap. 1 above.

5. Urbanus Regius in a letter to Erasmus, January 4, 1522. Allen, *Ep.* 1253.

6. On the 1511 edition, see Rice, "Humanist Idea of Christian Antiquity," Appendix 2.

7. Allen, *Ep.* 1289, line 18.

8. The preface to the Hilary edition which is in the form of a letter to Carondelet is Allen, *Ep.* 1334. See p. xvii, n. 2, above. In other correspondence of this period, Erasmus is at great pains to defend himself against his Louvain critics, and he refers to Carondelet as a supporter at court. See a letter to Carondelet in April 1522, *Ep.* 1276, and a lengthy letter to Mark Lauwerijns, dean of St. Donatian at Bruges, in February 1523, *Ep.* 1342. See also Allen III, p. 257, for a biographical note on Jean de Carondelet. The

actual copy of the edition which Erasmus inscribed and sent to Carondelet is now in the Houghton Library at Harvard.

9. The same complaints are expressed in P. Smulders, S.J., "Remarks on the Manuscript Tradition of the *De trinitate* of Saint Hilary of Poitiers'," *Studia Patristica* III.1 (Berlin, 1961), pp. 133–34.

10. For a translation of the *De trinitate*, see *Saint Hilary of Poitiers: The Trinity*, trans. Stephen McKenna, C.S.S.R., The Fathers of the Church (New York, 1954).

11. See Hilary's *De trinitate* 2.2–7.

12. Allen, *Ep.* 1334, lines 217–19.

13. Allen, *Ep.* 1334, lines 229–31. Several propositions from this portion of the preface were censured by the Sorbonne in 1526, and the faculty defended in its *censurae* the propriety of doctrinal definition and the value of scholastic theology. *Collectio judiciorum de novis erroribus*, ed. Charles du Plessis d'Argentré, 3 vols. (Paris, 1728–1736), II, 63, 76–77. A passage of several lines in this part was also obliterated at one time in the actual copy Erasmus had sent to Carondelet.

14. Allen, *Ep.* 1334, lines 362–81.

15. See Allen, *Ep.* 1350, lines 15–16. The latter half of the passage quoted, beginning with the words "The teachings of Christ," had at one time been obliterated in the copy Erasmus sent to Carondelet, though there is no reason to believe that Carondelet was responsible. He and Erasmus continued to have very cordial relations.

16. Hilary's failure to treat the Holy Spirit in *De trinitate* is also noted in the introduction to Father McKenna's English version, p. x. Erasmus' comments on this subject in the preface were vehemently criticized at Valladolid, Spain, in 1527 where, in a conference called to examine charges against him, Erasmus was accused of denying the Trinity and agreeing with the Arians. See Allen VI, p. 471, and Marcel Bataillon, *Erasme et l'Espagne* (Paris, 1937), chap. 5.

17. Allen, *Ep.* 1334, lines 451–53.

18. On this last point see also the introduction to McKenna's version of *De trinitate*, pp. x–xi.

19. "Ita fit ut, dum utrinque crudescit pugna, utrinque veritas amittatur." Allen, *Ep.* 1334, line 609.

20. Allen, *Ep*. 1334, lines 618–21. Cf. Is. 43:3, quoted in Matt. 12:20.
21. Allen, *Ep*. 1334, lines 834–36.
22. On Baechem and this appellation see Allen, *Ep*. 878, line 13.
23. Allen, *Ep*. 1334, lines 919–20, 927–28.
24. See notes 13, 16.

3
Erasmus and Aldus Manutius

ERASMUS SPENT MOST OF THE YEAR 1508 in Venice in close collaboration with the celebrated scholar-printer Aldus Manutius. It is an important episode in his life as well as in the broader history of Renaissance humanism. It is also interesting in the light it sheds on the relationship between author and printer in these early times, albeit in this case a unique relationship because of the character and stature of both men. Their meeting and joint endeavor took place in the course of an extended visit to Italy by Erasmus which in itself has several aspects of interest and importance. In this essay I shall focus on Erasmus' association with Aldus and his Press although without limiting myself solely to that central event. I want to see it in an ample context of its occasion and its times.

Erasmus first came to Italy, a land he had long desired to see, in the late summer of 1506. The opportunity for this journey arose while he was visiting England, where he had come several months earlier at the invitation of Lord Mountjoy, a former student and zealous patron of the humanist's, and at the urging of other friends. It was his second visit to England, and at this time especially he looked for the support and companionship he knew he would find there. After Italy England was his intellectual *patrie*, as Renaudet has observed,[1] and his English friends were both erudite and eminent. The precocious young lawyer Thomas More was foremost among them, as was John Colet, who had recently been appointed Dean of St. Paul's in London. Several others were scholars who had studied in Italy, notably at the University of Padua, and comprised the first generation of English humanists: William Grocyn, Thomas Linacre, William Latimer, Cuthbert Tunstall, William Lily. "There are indeed five or six men in London profoundly versed in Latin and Greek," Erasmus wrote, "and I doubt if Italy itself contains such good ones at this moment."[2]

The knowledge of Greek was one of their great accomplishments, and this linked Erasmus closely with them. Like Thomas More he had been striving in these early years for a mastery of the tongue.[3] It was the key to the most important literature of antiquity and above all to the study and the meaning of Holy Scripture, and was the indispensable tool for serious scholarship, as Erasmus recognized from the beginning.[4] He had recently translated Euripides' *Hecuba* into Latin verse as an exercise to test his skill in Greek, and now in London he was working on a second play of Euripides, *Iphigenia in Aulis*. (He translated from the first printed edition of Euripides' plays which Aldus Manutius had published in 1503.) He and Thomas More at the same time were translating a number of the dialogues of the Greek satirist Lucian. Lucian was a great favorite of both. "Whether you look for pleasure or edification," Erasmus declared, "there is not a comedy, or a satire, that challenges comparison with his dialogues."[5] He presented these translations in several instances as gifts to friends and potential patrons while he was in England. He offered one of the dialogues, *Toxaris*, to Richard Foxe, Bishop of Winchester, and he offered the *Hecuba* to William Warham, Archbishop of Canterbury and Lord Chancellor. Grocyn had introduced him to Warham at the prelate's Lambeth palace in London, and the meeting, the beginning of a long friendship, was a memorable one. Erasmus vividly describes it years later in the Botzheim Catalogue of his works.[6]

It was in the midst of these activities that the chance to go to Italy arose. It very likely occurred in April 1506 when

Erasmus was visiting Cambridge as a guest of John Fisher, Bishop of Rochester and Chancellor of the University.[7] He had applied to Cambridge for admission to take the degree of Doctor of Theology. In April, Henry VII and the royal court passed through the university town on their way to the shrine of Our Lady at Walsingham, and it is probable that Erasmus was offered the opportunity at that time. At any rate, the king's physician, Giovanni Battista Boerio, sought someone to accompany his two sons to Bologna to supervise their studies at the University there, and it was a post Erasmus accepted. He left England with the two young men and their tutor the beginning of June. It was a sudden decision, though Italy long had beckoned and was particularly attractive at this time in view of his desire to perfect his Greek and have access to the Greek legacy in all its fullness. "I came to Italy mainly in order to learn Greek," he said at the time, a statement he later expanded to embrace a broader purpose.[8] "To Italy alone I have journeyed of my own free will," he wrote in 1518, "partly to pay at least one visit to her holy places, partly to profit from the libraries of that part of the world and make acquaintance of its men of learning." In any event his friends urged him to go, and "as to the Promised land" he set out.

After a stormy crossing of the English Channel—from Dover to Calais took four days!—Erasmus and his companions reached Paris in mid-June. They remained there for nearly two months, an interval that gave Erasmus time to arrange for the publication of three books by Josse Bade Ascensius, a scholar-printer in Paris with whom he had previous ties. These editions (they appeared later that year after Erasmus had left Paris) were his translations of the *Hecuba* and *Iphigenia in Aulis*, which he dedicated to Archbishop Warham, his and More's translations of several dialogues of Lucian, which he dedicated individually to Bishop Foxe and other English friends, and a slightly enlarged version of his *Adagiorum collectanea*, which he dedicated to Lord Mountjoy.

This last work, a slim volume of proverbs, maxims, metaphors, etc., culled chiefly from Latin authors, had originally been published in 1500 in Paris by Johann Philipp.[9] It was Erasmus' first book. He now intended to expand it greatly and improve it, drawing extensively on the Greek sources he was now able to use. The second Paris edition was to be only an interim publication. In late August he and his party pressed on to Italy, traveling by way of Orleans and Lyons and across the Alps at Mont Cenis. They arrived in Turin, the seat of the Dukes of Savoy, in early September. As he rode on horseback through the Alps, Erasmus composed a poem on old age and its afflictions and surveyed nostalgically the swift passage of his own early years.[10] He was not yet forty, but he felt keenly that old age was upon him. Actually he was on the threshold of a long and extremely productive scholarly career, in the course of which the visit to Italy and especially to Venice was to be an important milestone. At Turin Erasmus obtained his doctorate in theology surprisingly within a few days. It was a degree he does not appear to have been too happy about, and he declared that it was not his own idea but that his friends had insisted upon it.[11] The party then continued its way to Bologna.

When they arrived there at the beginning of October, they found that Pope Julius II with the help of the French was preparing to lay siege to the city. Julius, who was restoring papal control throughout the Romagna, sought to oust the Bentivogli tyrant from Bologna and re-establish his own authority. Because of this threat Erasmus and his wards hastily withdrew to Florence and returned to Bologna only after the surrender of the city to the papal forces. Erasmus was back in time to witness the triumphal entry of the warrior Pope on November 11. The spectacle of the Roman Pontiff playing the role of Julius Caesar rather than vicar of Christ deeply shocked and scandalized him. It turned him into a pacifist, so it has been said.[12] Erasmus remained in Bologna until the end of 1507 when his mission of supervising the studies of the sons of Boerio was over. During this time he made the acquaintance of a distinguished scholar and professor at the University, Paolo Bombasio, and he resided in his home. Bombasio taught Greek and Latin, and we can assume that he counseled and assisted Erasmus in the work he was now pursuing, namely, his Greek studies and his revision and enlargement of the *Adagiorum collectanea*. Erasmus thought very highly of Bombasio's erudition as well as his personal charm.[13] Beatus Rhenanus, a later friend and colleague of Erasmus' and his first biographer, tells an interesting story about Erasmus in Bologna at this time.[14] Wearing the garb of an Augustinian canon, which included a white scapular, the great humanist was once mistaken for a plague doctor who wore a similar white cloth over the shoulders when on call. He had a rather alarming encounter: some youths threatened him with violence. Soon after, Erasmus petitioned Rome to be dispensed from wearing his religious habit and was given that permission provided he dressed as a priest.

Toward the end of his stay in Bologna Erasmus made contact with Aldus Manutius in Venice. On October 28 he wrote the famous printer to ask if he would publish his translations of the *Hecuba* and *Iphigenia in Aulis*.[15] His letter opens with glowing praise for Aldus' gifts and accomplishments, he inquires about some forthcoming work Aldus had planned (a Greek Plato, a polyglot Bible), he then broaches the subject of his translations. He tells Aldus that Bade had printed the two plays the year before and the entire edition had sold out, but that it was full of errors and he did not want Bade to reprint it. He would like Aldus to undertake a new and more correct edition in the italic type and small octavo format for which he had become renowned, and he declares that his own efforts would be given "immortality" if they were published in his magnificent type. In conclusion he suggests some possible business arrangements. He would furnish Aldus with his Latin text without recompense save for a few copies to present to his friends. He even spoke of paying for the publication or of taking a hundred or two hundred copies of the work. Aldus promptly replied and agreed to publish Erasmus' translations, and he apparently also invited Erasmus to come to Venice. Erasmus responded in a second letter to Aldus in November.[16] The bad weather and his poor health, he says, prevent him from making the journey, though he was anxious to visit him and discuss certain passages in the Greek text (Aldus had published it in 1503) that he had some doubts about. He indicates a few of these and suggests variant readings. (Erasmus in his own translations adopted the latter. Modern editors generally agree with Erasmus' corrections.) He also points out in the letter the difficulty of translating the various meters in Euripides' choruses and that he used fewer metrical patterns in his translations. He then stresses the hope that the book will be ready as soon as possible. He wants to have copies for his friends for New Year's Day, and he adds that he is going to Rome immediately after Christmas and wants copies for gifts there as well. He requests twenty or thirty copies and says he will make payment on delivery or, if Aldus wishes, will send it in advance. Finally, he sends along a new preface for the *Iphigenia* addressed to Archbishop Warham to replace the very brief one in the Bade edition. Aldus published the book, an 80-page octavo, in December. Further correspondence ensued, and Aldus now agreed to publish the new and expanded version of the *Adagiorum collectanea* Erasmus was working on. Thereupon, it appears, Erasmus gave up his intention of going to Rome and instead went to Venice in early January 1508 to work with Aldus on that edition.

The arrival of Erasmus in Venice has been given great significance. Its date is of primary importance, says Renaudet, in the history of Erasmus' intellectual and literary development and also, he continues, in the history of the human spirit.[17] Before we continue with this story, however, it is necessary to bring Aldus and the Venetian scene more fully into the picture. We have to know more about him and his work to understand his role. He was born in Bassiano south of Rome probably in 1452 and was considerably older than Erasmus. He had studied Latin and Greek in Rome and had become a teacher. In the 1480s he held the post of tutor to the princes of Carpi, Alberto and Lionello Pio, nephews of the famous scholar Pico della Mirandola. About 1490 he came to Venice and soon after began to prepare for the publishing enterprise that will establish his fame. His plan from the start was to make available all the important classic Greek authors. Without question Venice was the logical place to go, in Italy or anywhere in the West, to undertake so ambitious a project. The city was a commercial metropolis, it had a very active printing industry and hence technical expertise, it had a tradition of Greek studies and the prestigious University of Padua was close by, and it had a large émigré Greek community. Aldus later called it "a second Athens." Within a few years he became associated with Andrea Torresani d'Asola, a well-established and successful publisher who had been printing in Venice since 1472. In 1493 Torresani published a Latin grammar of Aldus', and by 1495 the two men had formed a partnership. At this point the Aldine Press, as we may call it, came into existence. It was a company capitalized by Torresani and Pier Francesco Barbarigo, the nephew of the doge, but with Aldus in charge of the all-important scholarly and editorial part of the business. Located *in aedibus Aldi Romani*, it soon became the most important and productive Press in Venice, perhaps in all of Europe. In 1505 Aldus married Torresani's daughter Maria, and, shortly after, he and the Press moved from its original location near the church of Sant' Agostino into the Torresani household on the other side of the Grand Canal near the church of San Paternian. It was to this address that Erasmus came when he arrived in Venice in early January.

Between 1495 and 1505 the Aldine Press produced more than one hundred editions, chiefly of the Greek classics but also of many Latin ones and of some notable Italian ones.[18]

A five-volume folio edition of Aristotle was its first great achievement. The works of Thucydides, Herodotus, Aristophanes, Sophocles, Euripides, Lucian, Homer, Demosthenes, and others soon followed, accompanied by Lucretius, Virgil, Horace, Juvenal, Cicero, Ovid, and others, and by Dante, Petrarch, and the letters of Saint Catherine of Siena. The years 1501–1503 were the busiest and most significant. 1501 saw the appearance of Aldus' famous octavo-size books set in a humanistic cursive or italic typeface, the production of which has been called revolutionary.[19] He gave the world handy portable editions of the major classical authors in a very agreeable and readable type. The first of these volumes were editions of Virgil and Horace in 1501; in 1502 and 1503 octavo editions in Greek cursive of the plays of Sophocles and Euripides were published. In 1502 the New Academy (or Aldine Academy) was formed, a group of scholars learned in Greek letters who were to advise and work with Aldus on the publication of his Greek texts.[20] Among its members were important émigré Greek scholars—Janus Lascaris, Marcus Musurus—as well as learned Italians—Scipio Carteromachus, Battista Egnazio, Pietro Bembo, Girolamo Aleandro. It was this academic circle whose conversations were conducted in Greek that Erasmus now joined in 1508. Although Aldus brought out no new books in 1506 and 1507 until he published Erasmus' translations of the two plays of Euripides, the Press was still in business, and Aldus after recovering from an illness was planning and preparing new editions. Erasmus' letter to him in October assumes as much, as does his arrival at the Aldine establishment. Beatus Rhenanus tells the story that when Erasmus came to the printing office he had to wait a long time before he was recognized and received.[21] Aldus found ordinary visitors an annoying interruption in his work. But when he discovered it was Erasmus, he was delighted, and he welcomed him as a guest in the home he shared with his father-in-law. Erasmus thus became a member of the lively community of workmen, scholars, and other associates of Aldus and Torresani, some thirty in number, which that household comprised. For the next nine or ten months Erasmus lived and worked there; he shared a room with one of the Aldine scholars, Girolamo Aleandro, a future cardinal and papal official of considerable importance. (Their paths crossed again many years later when the Lutheran controversy was dividing Europe, and hostile suspicions had disrupted their friendship.)

Erasmus has given us two descriptions (and several other references as well) of this Venetian scene. One is a very critical and satirical account that he published in 1531 in a colloquy entitled *Opulentia sordida*.[22] It is a diverting but devastating attack on Andrea Torresani as a stingy and miserly paterfamilias, and it describes living conditions in his household, particularly the bad food and wine he served, as wretched to an almost absurd degree. It is without a doubt a caricature, and it must be read as a lampoon in the context of later quarrels he had with Aleandro and Julius Caesar Scaliger. These need not concern us. From the skewed picture of life at the Torresani home, however, we get an impression that contains perhaps some slight element of truth and that allows us to extrapolate some information. But it certainly is not fair to Aldus and his publishing enterprise, and we know from other and better sources that Erasmus thought very highly of him and his work. The letter of October 28 bears witness to this, and so does the encomium he gives Aldus and his aims and achievements in the edition of the *Adagia* they published in 1508. This is in one of the most famous entries in that volume, the adage-essay *Festina lente*.[23] The adage means "Make haste slowly." Erasmus traces its ancient origin and sees it expressed by the anchor and dolphin emblem Aldus uses as his trademark. In a long passage he then extols the "tireless efforts" of this one man in restoring ancient learning, truly "a Herculean task," and he announces that "Aldus is building up a library which has no other limits than the world itself."

It is in another passage in this same adage-essay which Erasmus added years later that we have the other description of the Venetian scene that now engaged him. In it he describes in some detail the preparation of the Aldine *Adagia* and the great help Aldus and the scholars of the New Academy had so generously given him. His own words present a vivid picture:

> At the time when I, a Dutchman, was supervising the publication of my book of proverbs in Italy, every one of the scholars who were there offered me, without being asked, copies of authors which had never been printed, and which they thought I might be able to use. Aldus himself kept nothing back among his treasures. It was the same with Janus Lascaris, Battista Egnazio, Marcus Musurus, Frater Urbanus. I experienced the kindness of some whom I did not know either by sight or by name. I brought nothing with me to Venice but the raw material of a future work, as yet confused and undigested, and culled only from well-known authors. It was with great audacity on my part that set us both on, myself to write and Aldus to print. We broke the back of the work in nine months, more or less, and meanwhile I had had an encounter with a trouble I had not met before, the stone. Imagine how much of value I should have missed, if the scholars had not furnished me with manuscripts. Among these were the works of Plato in Greek, Plutarch's *Lives* and his *Moralia*, which began publication just as my work was ending; the *Deipnosophistai* of Atheneus, Aphthonius, Hermogenes with the commentary, the *Rhetoric* of Aristotle with the notes of Gregory Nazianzen; Aristides together with the notes, the little commentaries on Hesiod and Theocritus, the collection of proverbs which goes under the name of Plutarch, and the other called after Apostolius, which was lent me by Girolamo Aleandro. There were other less important things, which have either escaped my memory or need not be mentioned here. None of these had hitherto been printed.[24]

In a second adage-essay in the new *Adagia*, *Herculei labores*, "The Labors of Hercules," Erasmus expatiates at length on the "immense toil" and "infinite difficulties" he faced in compiling the book.[25] The task without question was immense, and it took nine months of constant and arduous work to bring it to completion. We can envisage the busy, noisy, even hectic scene in the printing office, Erasmus culling from the Greek sources that were now available to him and writing his text, Aldus and his printers running off the proofs and then the final folio sheets. The scene to be sure represents an important episode in Erasmus' life, and it is a memorable one in the annals of printing and of humanist scholarship.

The Aldine *Adagia* was published in September 1508. It was a vastly enlarged edition of the slim book of proverbs and other sayings that had been published in 1500 and reprinted with slight addition by Bade in 1506. It was now a folio volume of more than 500 pages. From 819 short entries in the original collection, it had grown to 3,260 entries, and its commentaries were more extended and included some longer essays. Its new title was *Adagiorum chiliades*, "Thousands of Adages," *chiliades tres ac centuriae fere totidem*, "three thousands and nearly as many hundreds," to be exact. What chiefly accounts for the expansion was the addition of proverbs and other references and passages from the Greek sources that Aldus and his scholars had made available.[26] This is its most distinctive character and its main importance in the history of humanism. It is a landmark book, the product of a most significant cultural and intellectual collaboration and the vehicle for the further extension and transmission of the heritage of ancient Greece. Margaret Mann Phillips has called it "in many ways a book of the new age, born to the sound of the printing press and impossible to imagine apart from the feverish excitement of the search for the living past."[27] It also marks an important stage in Erasmus' own career. It firmly established his reputation as Christendom's foremost scholar, and the work which had several later enlargements and editions became one of his most important contributions to the New Learning of this time.

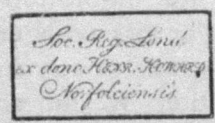

ERASMI ROTERODAMI ADAGIORVM
CHILIADES TRES, AC CENTV-
RIAE FERE TOTIDEM.

ALD. STVDIOSIS. S.

Quia nihil aliud cupio, q̃ prodesse uobis Studiosi. Cum uenisset in manus meas Erasmi Roterodami, hominis undecunq̃ doctiss. hoc adagioru opus eruditum, uarium, plenũ bonæ frugis,
& quod possit uel cum ipsa antiquitate certare, intermissis antiquis autorib. quos pa-
raueram excudendos, illud curauimus imprimendum, rati profuturum uobis
& multitudine ipsa adagioru quæ ex plurimis autorib. tam latinis, quàm
græcis studiose collegit summis certe laborib. summis uigiliis, &
multis locis apud utriusq̃ linguæ autores obiter uel correctis
acute, uel expositis erudite Docet præterea quot modis
ex hisce adagiis capere utilitatem liceat, puta quẽ-
admodum ad uarios usus accõmodari pos-
sint. Adde, qđ circiter decẽ millia uer-
suum ex Homero Euripide, & cæ-
teris Græcis eodẽ metro in
hoc opere fideliter, &
docte tralata ha
bẽtur, præ
ter plu
rima
ex Pla-
tone, De-
mosthene, & id
genus ali
is. An
autem uerus sim,
ἴδοι ὁ λύσας, ἴδοι καὶ τὸ πλέγμα.
Nam, quod dicitur, αὐτὸς αὐτὸν αὐλῶ.

Præponitur hisce adagiis duplex index Alter secundum literas
alphabeti nostri. nam quæ græca sunt, latina quoq̃
habentur. Alter per capita rerum.

Title page of the Aldine (1508) edition of Erasmus' *Adagia*.
The Pierpont Morgan Library.

Erasmus stayed on in Venice for a month or two after the publication of the *Adagiorum chiliades*. He helped Aldus proofread a Greek edition of Plutarch's *Moralia*, which was published in March 1509, and he worked on texts of the comedies of Terence and Plautus and the tragedies of Seneca Aldus was preparing for future publication. Doubtless, the other Aldine editions which appeared at this time—Pliny's *Letters* in November 1508 and a two-volume *Rhetores Graeci* in November 1508 and May 1509—came under discussion. Aldus reciprocated the very high opinion Erasmus had of him and would have sought his aid and advice. In late 1508 Erasmus left Venice for nearby Padua where he visited the learned Marcus Musurus, professor of Greek at the University and a member of the Aldine circle. He had helped Erasmus extensively on the Greek manuscripts he was consulting, and Beatus Rhenanus in his life of Erasmus gives him high praise in this connection.[28] He had read everything, he declares, and there was nothing he could not explain or disentangle. While he was in Padua, Erasmus accepted the post of tutor of rhetoric to the young Alexander Stewart, the natural son of James IV of Scotland, who was a student at the University. Not long after, however, the imminence of war in northern Italy caused Erasmus and his royal pupil to move south, first to Ferrara, then to Siena. The League of Cambrai, a coalition of all the great powers and several smaller ones against Venice, had been formed in December, and the invasion of the Veneto now loomed. (The Venetians suffered a crushing defeat by the French at Agnadello in May 1509. One immediate consequence was the closing of the Aldine Press until 1512 and Aldus' departure for Ferrara.)

Once he had settled Alexander Stewart in his studies in Siena, Erasmus took leave of him and in early 1509 went to Rome. It was inevitable that he make such a trip. Whatever his misgivings about the militant Pope, Rome was the *caput mundi*, the eternal city, "the most famous city in the world," as he called it, and its monuments of antiquity and other sites of interest as well as its libraries and its scholars drew him there.[29] It was a Rome now beginning to be adorned with the greatest works of the High Renaissance. Julius was an ardent and lavish Maecenas, and it was at his orders that the new Basilica of Saint Peter's was begun in 1506 under Bramante's direction, that Michelangelo began painting the ceiling of the Sistine Chapel in late autumn 1508, and that Raphael at the same time began his immortal frescoes in the *Stanze* of the Vatican Palace. Erasmus was there at that incredible moment, and one wonders if he was aware of what was now in progress. It was a Rome, too, in the throes of diplomatic negotiation and debate over relations with Venice and the question of joining the League of Cambrai against her.[30] Julius did join the coalition against Venice in March 1509, and Erasmus tells us that his view on this important issue was canvassed by the Pope. This may come as a surprise, given the conventional image of Erasmus as a kind of nemesis of the warlike Julius, but here is his own account in the Botzheim Catalogue:

> When I was living in Rome, to please Raffaele, Cardinal of San Giorgio, I wrote a speech against the proposal to declare war on Venice, for which he asked me in Julius' name, for the question was then under discussion in the sacred college. I then put the opposite case; and the second speech won the day, although I had spent more time on the first and written it more from the heart.[31]

The Raffaele Erasmus refers to is Cardinal Raffaele Riario, a cousin of the Pope's and one of the most prominent prelates in Rome. Erasmus notes in his *Compendium vitae* that when he was in Rome the Cardinal "especially was kind" to him.[32]

Erasmus' stay in Rome in the early months of 1509 was not long, but there is every indication it was an agreeable one. "It is impossible to describe," writes Beatus Rhenanus, "with what great applause and with what great joy he was received there among the cultured."[33] These included many of the most eminent cardinals and prelates: Cardinal Riario, Cardinal Giovanni de' Medici who would succeed Julius a few years hence as Leo X, the Venetian Cardinal Domenico Grimani, Egidio da Viterbo, general of the Augustinians and a distinguished scholar himself, Tommaso Inghirami, prefect of the Vatican library. Cardinal Grimani, who had an extensive library especially rich in Greek manuscripts, tried to persuade him to remain in Rome, and he was offered a curial post which would lead to higher dignities in the future.[34] Erasmus was sorely tempted, but by July he had decided to return to England, his "adopted" home. Before that decision, however, Erasmus went back to Siena and brought his young ward to Rome for a visit incognito and then on a trip further south to see the cave of the Cumaean Sibyl, a place famed for Aeneas' dramatic visit there. It was shortly after this excursion that Alexander Stewart was summoned home to Scotland by his father (he was killed in the battle of Flodden Field in 1513) and Erasmus received the messages that brought him back to England.

These messages were letters from Lord Mountjoy and Archbishop Warham urging him to return at once to enjoy the benefactions that would be his in the new reign that had now begun.[35] They announced the succession of the youthful Henry VIII, who succeeded to the throne on the death of his father in April 1509 and heralded a new era of largesse for learning and scholarship now at hand. "Heaven smiles, earth rejoices; all is milk and honey and nectar," Mountjoy proclaimed. "Tight-fistedness is well and truly banished. Generosity scatters wealth with unstinting hand." Warham promised a benefice and other rewards and wanted Erasmus to spend the rest of his life in England. The new king, of course, was a friend and knew Erasmus well. The great humanist's expectations now ran exceedingly high. He later wrote Cardinal Grimani: "It was to England that the ties of old and dear acquaintance, the very generous promises of influential friends, and the very favorable attitude of a most successful king all summoned me."[36] And so sometime in July 1509 he left Rome and journeyed north. His trip took him across the central Alps this time by the Splügen pass into Switzerland at Chur and then on to Constance and Strasbourg and down the Rhine to the Low Countries and across to England. It was a long and difficult journey. As he rode on horseback on his Alpine route he meditated on the world he had seen, with its vanity and folly, and in thinking of his wise and witty friend Thomas More the idea for his most famous book came into his mind, *Moriae encomium*. "I was inspired by your surname of More, which is as close in form to *Moria* (Folly) as you are in fact remote from folly itself."[37] This "flight of fancy" became his masterpiece of humor, irony, and biting satire, *The Praise of Folly*. He dashed it off soon after he arrived at More's home in Bucklersbury in the heart of London as he recuperated from his travels and from another attack of the kidney stone, and he dedicated it to his Lucianic collaborator and closest friend, Thomas More.

The return to England was not so rewarding as he had anticipated. He remained there, however, for nearly five years, the first two of which are almost completely hidden from view. There is a mysterious gap in his correspondence for this latter period. We know he came to More's home in London on his return from Italy; we next hear from him enroute to Paris in the spring of 1511 to arrange for the printing of *The Praise of Folly*. The intervening months are a blank. We can assume they were spent congenially with his English friends and in productive scholarly work. After that he went to Cambridge where he taught Greek and lectured on Saint Jerome. His scholarly endeavors were pursued, but he had many complaints about life at Cambridge, and the high hopes that had brought him back to England in 1509 had not been realized. In early 1514 he left Cambridge, and that summer he bade farewell to England. Crossing to the continent he made his way to Basel where he joined forces with another famous printer, Johann Froben, and established ties that were even more intimate and far more enduring than those he had with Aldus Manutius.

NOTES

1. Augustin Renaudet, *Erasme et l'Italie* (Geneva, 1954), p. 41.
2. CWE 2, Letter 185.
3. Erika Rummel, *Erasmus as a Translator of the Classics* (Toronto, 1985), pp. 3ff.
4. CWE 2, Letter 149.
5. CWE 2, Letter 193; see also CWE 9, pp. 301–302.
6. CWE 9, pp. 297–98; see also CWE 2, Letter 188.
7. Allen I, Appendix VI.
8. CWE 2, Letter 203; CWE 5, Letter 809.
9. See Margaret Mann Phillips, *The 'Adages' of Erasmus: A Study with Translations* (Cambridge, 1964), chap. 2.
10. CWE 85, pp. 12–25.
11. CWE 2, Letters 200, 201.
12. Phillips, *'Adages' of Erasmus*, p. 105.
13. Adage I.vi.1.
14. CHR³, p. 51.
15. CWE 2, Letter 207.
16. CWE 2, Letter 209.
17. Renaudet, *Erasme et l'Italie*, p. 83. See also Deno John Geanakoplos, *Byzantium and the Renaissance* (Hamden, Conn., 1973), chap. 9 (this work was originally entitled *Greek Scholars in Venice*).
18. Manlio Dazzi, *Aldo Manuzio e il Dialogo Veneziano di Erasmo* (Vicenza, 1969), pp. 209–19. See also Martin Lowry, *The World of Aldus Manutius* (Ithaca, N.Y., 1979), chap. 4.
19. Harry George Fletcher III, *New Aldine Studies* (San Francisco, 1988), pp. 4–6.
20. Geanakoplos, *Byzantium and the Renaissance*, pp. 128–32.
21. CHR³, pp. 52–53.
22. *The Colloquies of Erasmus*, trans. Craig R. Thompson (Chicago, 1965), pp. 488–99. The English title in this edition is "Penny-Pinching." See also Phillips, *'Adages' of Erasmus*, pp. 62–69.
23. Adage II.i.1. It is translated in Phillips, *'Adages' of Erasmus*, pp. 171–90.

24. Ibid., pp. 185–86. This account is in a passage added in 1526.

25. Adage III.i.1. It is translated in ibid., pp. 190–209. The two adage-essays are the longest in the 1508 edition of the *Adagia*, and each begins a new grouping of a thousand entries.

26. Geanakoplos, *Byzantium and the Renaissance*, pp. 272–73.

27. Phillips, *'Adages' of Erasmus*, p. 72.

28. CHR³, pp. 52–53.

29. CWE 3, p. 94.

30. Ludwig Pastor, *History of the Popes from the Close of the Middle Ages*, trans. F. I. Antrobus et al., 41 vols. (St. Louis, 1891–1953), VI, 290ff.

31. CWE 9, p. 351.

32. CHR³, p. 44.

33. CHR³, p. 53.

34. CWE 3, Letter 334, and CHR³, pp. 53–54.

35. CWE 2, Letters 214, 215.

36. CWE 2, Letter 334.

37. CWE 2, Letter 222. See also John C. Olin, *Six Essays on Erasmus* (New York, 1979), chap. 4, "*The Praise of Folly*," pp. 49–56.

4

Erasmus' *Adagia* and More's *Utopia*

In memoriam Margaret Mann Phillips

MONTAIGNE REMARKED IN HIS ESSAY "On Repentance" that if he had met Erasmus he would have expected him to speak in proverbs. He was thinking most probably of the collection Erasmus had gathered from the ancient classics and had published in numerous editions, the *Adagia*, or, more descriptively, the *Adagiorum chiliades*, "thousands of adages," containing not only the proverbs themselves, but also essays, long and short, explaining the proverbs, recounting their literary sources, and enunciating themes dear to the heart of Erasmus.[1] Indeed, it can be called at least in part a book of essays, and although they are of a different character and tone from Montaigne's, there is some kinship perhaps in the genre.

I am going to translate here one of the shorter adage-essays and comment on it. My purpose is to call attention to a significant theme in the reform humanism Erasmus represented. I am struck by the affinity between this theme and that great masterpiece of the Renaissance, Thomas More's *Utopia*, and I want particularly to discuss the character and significance of their relationship.

The *Adagia* saw many editions and revisions during Erasmus' lifetime. First published in Paris in 1500 at the outset of his career, it was greatly expanded in 1508 and published in Venice by the famous printer Aldus Manutius with whom Erasmus was working at that time. The next important edition, further revised and enlarged, appeared in 1515, issuing from the press of Johann Froben in Basel where Erasmus had recently gone and where he was henceforth regularly to publish. This revised *Adagia* has been called the "Utopian" edition because of the affinity of several themes prominent in it with Thomas More's *Utopia*, which was first published in 1516.[2] There were several subsequent Froben editions of the *Adagia* while Erasmus lived and many reprints both during and after his lifetime. The volume grew to be a formidable collection of 4,151 adages, a vast treasure house of classical erudition and a compendium of Erasmian comments, opinions, and critiques.

The adage-essay that I have selected for translation and discussion here is the first one in the collection, the proverb *Amicorum communia omnia*, "Friends have all things in common." In essay form it dates from the 1508 Aldine edition, and there are significant additions to it in the 1515 and 1526 Froben editions. It had appeared in embryo in the Paris edition of 1500, but it became proverb number one only in the expanded edition of 1508, a place of honor and importance it retained thereafter. Let me now present the English translation of the complete text.[3]

Friends Have All Things in Common

Τὰ τῶν φίλων χοινὰ, that is, Friends have all things in common. Since there is no proverb more wholesome or more famous I have chosen it as a good omen to begin this book of adages. And indeed if it were as fixed in the hearts of men as it is ever on their lips, certainly most of the evils of our life would be averted. Socrates inferred from this proverb that all things belong to good men just as they do to the gods. For all things belong to the gods, he said. Good men are the friends of the gods, and friends have all things in common. Therefore, good men possess all things.

The proverb is quoted in Euripides' *Orestes*, *Phoenissae*, and

Andromache, and in Terence's *Adelphoe*. It is said that it was also in Menander's play of the same name. Cicero quotes it in the first book of the *De officiis*, and Aristotle cites it in Book VIII of the *Ethics* and Plato in Book V of the *Laws*. In the latter passage Plato attempts to show that the best state of the commonwealth consists in the sharing of all things. "The first society then," he declares, "the one with the best constitution and laws, is where the old saying will be observed as far as possible throughout the whole society. I mean the saying that friends have all their possessions in common." *He also says that a society will be happy and blessed where the words 'mine' and 'not mine' are never heard. But it is amazing how displeasing, yes, how hateful that community of Plato's is to Christians, although nothing ever said by a pagan philosopher is more in keeping with the mind of Christ.*[4]

Aristotle in Book II of the Politics *modifies the view of Plato, saying that ownership and property belong to specific individuals but otherwise for the sake of use, virtue, and civil fellowship everything is common according to the proverb.*[5] Martial in Book II of the *Epigrams* jests about someone called Candidus who always had this adage on his lips although he shared nothing with his friends:

> Candidus, O Candidus, pompously you echo this adage
> Night and day, "Friends have all in common."

And he concludes his epigram:

> You give naught away, yet you say, O Candidus,
> "Friends share all."

Theophrastus in Plutarch's essay "On Brotherly Love" elegantly remarks: "If the goods of friends are held in common, it is very fitting that the friends of friends also be shared in common."

Cicero in the first book of the *Laws* seems to attribute this adage to Pythagoras when he says: "For whence comes that Pythagorean dictum, the goods of friends are held in common and friendship is equality." Moreover, Diogenes Laertius has Timaeus relate that this saying had its origin with

Pythagoras. *Aulus Gellius in his* Attic Nights, *Book I, chapter 9, claims that Pythagoras not only was the author of this proverb but also introduced a community of life and resources, even such as Christ wishes all Christians to practice. For whoever Pythagoras had admitted into that band of his disciples gave whatever money and property they possessed to the common fund. This practice is called in Latin* coenobium, *a word undoubtedly derived from the fellowship of life and possessions.*[6]

The development of this adage-essay is remarkable. In 1500 Erasmus had limited himself to a few lines. He simply stated that the proverb was quoted by a character in one of Terence's plays and was cited also in Plato "under the name of Euripides." In 1508 a major expansion of its classical sources took place, and drawing on Cicero and Diogenes Laertius Erasmus attributes its origin to Pythagoras. In 1515 came further revision. Several new sentences were added which radically changed the character of the essay. The adage now took on greater thrust as a reform concept, and by the same token its affinity with the teachings of Christ was affirmed. The correspondence of its presentation in such incisive form in this edition with More's description (and Hythloday's defense) of Utopian society is also striking. More's book in fact, we might say, is a dramatic commentary on this adage. And the emphatic references to what Christ thought and desired not only heighten the proverb's role as a principle of moral and social reform but demonstrate that harmony between the classical heritage and Christianity which Erasmus and other humanists perceived. Finally in 1526 Erasmus somewhat qualified the full Platonic ideal of community by adding a restraining note from Aristotle. He retreated slightly, it would seem, though his citation from the *Politics* hardly does justice to the fundamental critique which the great Peripatetic launched against his former teacher's communalism.

The theme of this adage-essay and its correspondence with More's *Utopia*, as I have indicated, especially intrigue me.

Statue of Thomas More outside Chelsea Old Church, England. Photo by author.

Both Erasmus and More present and develop the same basic idea: the best social order is one in which all possessions are held in common and a close community of living and sharing prevails. Both men appear most certainly to be advocating communism, albeit without the Marxist dialectic or any modern political overtone. They are aware that their prescription has its roots in classical as well as Christian antiquity—a factor, it would seem, that makes it an integral part of their humanist inheritance. The question I should now like to pose is how should we understand this espousal of so radical a moral and social concept, how literally should we take it as a reform proposal.

The question is often asked of More's *Utopia*, but it is one not easily or definitely answered in view of the character of that work—its fictive as well as its dialogue form, its occasional irony, the ambiguity of its proper names. Is Utopia really Noplace? Is Hythloday simply spinning a yarn? If not, what lesson are we to draw from this "best state of a commonwealth"? That question perhaps can be better approached through Erasmus's *Adagia*. If the same theme is struck in both works, the more direct and straightforward expression of it should be the simpler to analyze, the clearer to grasp.

In the introduction to the *Adagia* which first appeared in the Aldine edition of 1508 Erasmus discusses the nature and use of proverbs, and to show how a very short adage can contain deep philosophical and religious truths he cites the dictum "Friends have all things in common." His extended comment proving this point runs as follows:[7]

> If anyone more diligently and deeply analyzes that saying of Pythagoras "Friends have all things in common," he will certainly find the sum and substance of human happiness expressed in this brief remark. What else is Plato driving at in so many volumes save to promote community and its foundation, friendship? If he could convince mortals of these things, war, envy, fraud would immediately depart from our

midst; in short, a whole army of evils would march out of our lives once for all. What other aim had Christ, the prince of our religion? Truly He gave to the world only one precept, the rule of charity, and He stressed that everything in the Law and the Prophets hangs on that alone. Or, what else does charity urge save that all have all things in common? Namely, it urges that, joined in friendship with Christ and bound to Him by the same force that unites Him with the Father, and imitating as far as we can that perfect communion by which He and the Father are one, we also become one with Him and, as Paul says, are made one spirit and one flesh in God, so that by right of friendship all that is His is shared with us and all that is ours is shared with Him. Then it urges that, joined with one another in equal bonds of friendship as members of the same Head, as one and the same body, we come alive with the same spirit and weep and rejoice at the same things. That mystical bread gathered from many grains into one flour also reminds us of this, as does the draught of wine fused into one liquid from the clusters of many grapes. Finally, charity urges that, since the sum total of all created things is in God and God in turn is in all things, the whole universe, as it were, be restored to unity. You see what an ocean of philosophy or, rather, theology has been opened up for us by so small a proverb.

What strikes us most about this explanation of Erasmus' is how he relates the proverb to Scripture and to basic Christian doctrine. In the adage-essay of 1515 he had indicated that the Platonic–Pythagorean dictum was in harmony with the teaching of Christ, but here seven years earlier he had spelled out that agreement in considerable detail. (These introductory remarks of course prefaced the adage-essay in 1508.) Plato's *communitas* is equated with Christ's *charitas*, and the peace and well-being of society is made to coincide with membership in the mystical body of Christ and with universal reconciliation, of both of which St. Paul so often speaks.[8] The proverb is given a fundamentally religious meaning, or at least its social thrust is confirmed and reinforced by religion and rooted in a profound theology of unity.[9] It is an impressive statement. It is clear proof, I think, of Erasmus' religious seriousness and depth, and it corroborates an observation of John O'Malley's that the doctrine of the mystical body of Christ "must be taken as one of the fundamental strands in the fabric of this thought."[10]

What does this explanation tell us about this axiomatic prescription as a social reform, about Utopian communism as an example to imitate? I think we begin to realize that what both Erasmus and More are presenting is an ultimate moral and religious ideal—a way of life millenial, or practically so, in its fulfillment of the demands of Christian charity and its achievement of that unity for which Christ prayed. The pagans with the light of reason may have glimpsed the possibility and may even have elaborated their vision, but its actual attainment will be the product of Christian virtue and brotherhood as it is the object of Christian hope. This seems to be the message Erasmus conveys in his introductory remarks. More in *Utopia* is not so explicit, but his work lends itself to this understanding.

A true expert on *Utopia*, Edward Surtz, interprets More's attitude in this way.[11] In his view Utopia is an ideal that exists only in More's mind and heart, and its realization must depend on the moral rectitude of those who would create and maintain such a commonwealth. More's "ideal will always remain that of a common Christian life for a whole Christian nation, but the realization of this ideal depends upon the character of its citizens, who must be perfect in their Christianity—or as eager in their pursuit of Christian perfection—as the Utopians are in their rationality."[12] That's a tall order indeed. Such perfection on a broad scale, whether Christian or rational, is out of reach, for the nature itself of man and the conditions of his earthbound existence stand in the way. The Utopian ideal then is a millenial dream; the concrete circumstances and practical problems of man in society require other arrangements.

Does this interpretation render *Utopia* as well as Erasmus' adage-essay a futile, not to say meaningless, exercise? I think not, but before I answer that question I want to say a few more words about More's famous book. I would like to take note of three passages in *Utopia* that are particularly relevant, I believe, to what we have been discussing.

In Book II of *Utopia* in the description of Utopian religions we are told that when the citizens of that mythical commonwealth heard about Christ and His teaching many were disposed to become Christian.[13] Hythloday, More's narrator, speculates that it may have been "because they thought it [Christianity] nearest to that belief which has the widest prevalence among them." And he adds: "But I think that this factor, too, was of no small weight, that they had heard that His disciples' common way of life had been pleasing to Christ and that it is still in use among the truest societies of Christians."[14] This comment echoes especially the concluding remarks that Erasmus added to his adage-essay in 1515. The whole passage of course asserts the affinity between pagan, that is, rational, and Christian ideals insofar as the Utopian scheme of things is concerned.

A similar point is made in a passage near the end of *Utopia*, though an extremely interesting qualification is appended which underlines the difficulty in making good the ideal. Hythloday, summing up the communal order that prevails in Utopia, declares:

> Nor does it occur to me to doubt that a man's regard for his own interests or the authority of Christ our Saviour—who in His wisdom could not fail to know what was best and who in His goodness could not fail to counsel what He knew to be best—would long ago have brought the whole world to adopt the laws of the Utopian commonwealth, had not one single monster, the chief and progenitor of all plagues, striven against it—I mean, Pride.[15]

The linkage of Utopia with a Christian paradigm is asserted, but the great stumbling block is seen as man himself—his imperfection, his sinfulness. "This serpent from hell," Hythloday continues, "entwines itself around the hearts of men and acts like the suckfish in preventing and hindering them from entering on a better way of life."[16]

This realism finds even more pointed expression in a memorable and oft-quoted passage in Book I. In the dialogue that is the central theme of that Book about serving as a councilor to a prince, More counters Hythloday's high-minded disdain for such a post with these remarks:

> So it is in the commonwealth. So it is in the deliberations of monarchs. If you cannot pluck up wrongheaded opinions by the root, if you cannot cure according to your heart's desire vices of long standing, yet you must not on that account desert the commonwealth. You must not abandon the ship in a storm because you cannot control the winds. On the other hand, you must not force upon people new and strange ideas which you realize will carry no weight with persons of opposite conviction. On the contrary, by the indirect approach you must seek and strive to the best of your power to handle matters tactfully. What you cannot turn to good you must make as little bad as you can. For it is impossible that all should be well unless all men were good, a situation which I do not expect for a great many years to come.[17]

Hythloday objects and makes his reply, but More's hardheaded and pragmatic approach to political reality in this instance is certainly striking and has the ring of simple truth. "The author of *Utopia* was no Utopian," observes Professor Hexter in discussing this remarkable passage.[18] It is the last sentence, however, to which I would like to call attention: "It is impossible that all should be well unless all men were good. . . ." Since they are not and their vices like the suckfish hold them back, the Utopian dream per se is unrealizable. What then is its purpose? Why do More and Erasmus both advance this lofty ideal?

I have already stressed that the ideal they have in mind is a spiritual one. It has to do with men being good; it has to do with Christ's command to love one another; it has to do with the values men live by; it has to do with changing and reforming lives. Obviously, the social dimension is paramount. The health of society depends on how men behave. Greedy landlords, ambitious princes, fawning courtiers cause suffering and disorder. It is they who bear the brunt of the criticism in the first Book of *Utopia*, and it is their absence in the commonwealth described in the second Book that makes that happy land Utopia. There the vices so prevalent in the Europe of More's time have been eradicated. Utopian laws and institutions supposedly have eliminated them, but it is actually the moral philosophy of the Utopians and their many virtues that have triumphed. Good people have built a good society. More's message, I think, is contained therein. Erasmus wrote that More "published *Utopia* to show what the cause of our civil problems are, having England which he knows and understands so well particularly in mind."[19] The conciseness and precision of that statement are admirable. If we read it in the context of what both men have written, it means that the causes lie within man himself and that a better world awaits man's moral reformation. It means that the redress of the social and political ills besetting Christian Europe in those critical times will only proceed from a change of heart in its peoples. More has dramatized that theme in *Utopia*; Erasmus has expounded it with special emphasis in the *Adagia*. Together they have raised a beacon on the margin of a stormy sea.

Notes

1. Margaret Mann Phillips, *The 'Adages' of Erasmus: A Study with Translations* (Cambridge, 1964). See also Thomas M. Greene, "Erasmus's 'Festina lente': Vulnerabilities of the Humanist Text," in *Mimesis: From Mirror to Method, Augustine to Descartes*, edd. John D. Lyons and Stephen G. Nichols, Jr. (Hanover and London,

1982), pp. 132–48. The first 500 adages have been translated and published in CWE 31: *Adages Iii to Iv100*, trans. Margaret Mann Phillips, annotated by R. A. B. Mynors (Toronto, 1982). The complete *Adagia* is in the second volume of the Leiden *Opera omnia* of Erasmus (1703–1706). A new critical edition will appear in the Amsterdam *Opera omnia*, now in progress.

2. Phillips, *'Adages' of Erasmus*, pp. 106ff. More began writing *Utopia* at Antwerp in the summer of 1515 and finished the book in London the following year. Erasmus arranged for its publication by Dirk Martens at Louvain later that year. See J. H. Hexter, *More's* UTOPIA (Princeton, 1952), pp. 15ff.

3. I have used the text in the *Adagiorum chiliades* published by the heirs of Sebastian Gryphius at Lyons in 1559. Additions to the text as it was expanded and revised by Erasmus in earlier editions are in italics and are noted. I have not always repeated in my translation the proverb as quoted by Erasmus from the ancient author he cites.

4. The above two sentences in italics were added in the 1515 Froben edition. The second citation is from the *Republic*, Book V (462c).

5. This sentence in italics was added in the 1526 Froben edition. Book II of Aristotle's *Politics* contains an extensive critique of Plato's community ideal. Chapter 5 of Book II is especially relevant here.

6. The above three sentences in italics were added in the 1515 Froben edition. The term *coenobium* which Erasmus also gives in its Greek form χοινόβιον literally means "common life."

7. I have made the translation from the 1559 Lyons edition, col. 11. The text is the same as the original 1508 text.

8. Rom 12:4–5, 1 Cor. 12:12–27, Eph. 1:9–10, Col. 1:20.

9. See John 17:20–23.

10. In "Erasmus and Luther, Continuity and Discontinuity as Key to Their Conflict," *Sixteenth Century Journal*, 5, No. 2 (October 1974), 55.

11. In "Thomas More and Communism: The Solution," *The Praise of Pleasure* (Cambridge, Mass., 1957), chap. 15.

12. Ibid., p. 182.

13. St. Thomas More, *Utopia*, The Complete Works of Thomas

More 4, edd. Edward Surtz, s.j., and J. H. Hexter (New Haven, 1964), pp. 217–19. Hereafter cited as CW 4.

14. The reference is to Acts 2:42–45 and 4:32–37, the *locus classicus* for the existence of a community of goods, a χοινωνία, among early Christians, and also to religious orders who practiced a community life.

15. CW 4, p. 243.

16. CW 4, pp. 243–45.

17. CW 4, pp. 99–101. German Arciniegas hits the bull's-eye when he states in his *America in Europe: A History of the New World in Reverse*, trans. Gabriela Arciniegas and R. Victoria Arana (New York, 1986), p. 54, that "Utopia presupposes a government in the hands of good men." Chapter 3 of this work presents an excellent discussion of More's classic in its historical context.

18. *More's* UTOPIA, p. 131.

19. My translation of Erasmus' reference to Utopia in the sketch of Thomas More he wrote in a letter to Ulrich von Hutten July 23, 1519, Allen, *Ep.* 999, lines 256–59.

5
More, Montaigne, and Matthew Arnold: Thoughts on the Utopian Vision

I INTEND TO DISCUSS several utopias of a more or less literary character that are not usually considered in the conventional listing of utopian projects. Thomas More's famous masterpiece which gives us the word we use to designate the entire genre can be studied both as a project and as something far more penetrating and profound. Like Plato's *Republic* it is a classic on every score, and I shall use it as a standard, so to speak, a basis for comparing or contrasting the other utopias I shall describe. My title indicates that Montaigne and Matthew Arnold will come under scrutiny insofar as they offer somewhere in their work a "utopian vision." I must hasten to add three other names to my heading: Rabelais, Jonathan Swift, and Voltaire. For the sake of brevity and an alliterative rhythm I left their names out of my title, but their contribution to the utopian literary corpus is equally great, and in this essay, if not in its title, they will receive their due.

My procedure will be to treat these authors in chronological order—Rabelais, Montaigne, Swift, Voltaire, Matthew Arnold. Their utopias will be briefly described, and my thoughts about them and how they relate to More's *Utopia* will follow. At the outset let me say a few words about the famous book of Thomas More.

More's *Utopia*—the word means "No place"—is an imaginative dialogue between More and a Portuguese sailor, Raphael Hythloday, who had been to the New World with Amerigo Vespucci and has returned with an amazing story to tell about an ideal commonwealth he visited there. The work is divided into two very different parts or books. In Book I More and Hythloday discuss the many ills and injustices prevalent in the England and Europe of their time. In Book II Hythloday describes the ideal commonwealth of Utopia where the vices that plague Christendom have largely been eradicated. The social order responsible for this, Hythloday insists, is communism, that is, a society in which there is no private property and all things are held and shared in common. The two Books are marvelously complementary; they analyze two contrasting social and political orders whose stark comparison cannot fail to heighten perception and stimulate thought about our human relations and the morality or lack of it which governs them. The work raises many issues and has interpretive problems, but its main thrust, its basic message, I think, is clear enough. It is a moral one: good people have made a good society. More is talking about the values men live by, and he is saying that the well-being of a society depends on how men behave. It is a moral, even a religious, ideal, not a social blueprint, that he is presenting.[1] He is "a man of conscience," not a social ideologue, in this classic work. Let me turn now to the other utopias I want to discuss.

François Rabelais is first on the list. His utopia is described in the First Book of his famous work, the Book called *Gargantua* which relates the life and exploits of that fantastic giant. It first saw the light of day in 1534; More's *Utopia* had originally been published in 1516. Rabelais knew More's book—he was a disciple of the humanism sweeping Europe at this time—but the idealized community he describes in *Gargantua* is of a very different type from the model commonwealth of More. Erasmus was Rabelais' mentor, and it is the influence of the great Dutch humanist that can be observed in that utopian segment of the First Book I am referring to.[2] Those chapters tell the story of the fabulous Abbey of Thélème, a most unusual monastery which Gargantua established and endowed.

To call Thélème most unusual is an understatement. It is a religious community whose features, practices, and total ambiance are the exact opposite of everything characteristic of religious life in Rabelais' day and traditionally as well. Gargantua instituted a religious order that was completely contrary to all others. There are no regulations, no daily routine, no vows at Thélème. Both men and ladies are admitted, though only those of handsome physique and the right disposition. There is no compulsion to remain. Thélème's monks and nuns dress elegantly "according to their own taste and pleasure." They live in magnificent and pleasurable surroundings, to say the least. Their rule has only one clause: Do what you will. Let me quote from the chapter explaining that injunction:

> All their life was regulated not by laws, statutes, or rules, but according to their own free will and pleasure. They arose from bed when they pleased, and drank, ate, worked, and slept when the fancy seized them. Nobody woke them: nobody compelled them to eat or to drink, or to do anything else whatever. So it was that Gargantua had established it. In their rule there was only one clause:
> DO WHAT YOU WILL
> because people who are free, well-born, well-bred, and easy in honest company have a natural spur and instinct which drives them to virtuous deeds and deflects them from vice; and this they called honor.

Freedom is the keynote of the Abbey of Thélème. The word Thélème, like Utopia, is a Greek derivative and means "free will." The startling rule of the Abbey echoes St. Augustine's "Love and do as you will." Rabelais has translated this to mean that those who are well-born and well-bred will by natural instinct and free choice live virtuous lives. In the Abbey they can be left to their own devices. This presupposes, of course, that those who enter the monastery are the right type. A careful screening then must occur, and this is provided for at the great entrance gate of the Abbey. Above the gate is a lengthy inscription stating in detail who may and who may not enter therein. Hypocrites and bigots, greedy lawyers and miserly usurers, gluttons and lechers, and many others are forbidden entrance. But worthy gentlemen "from every coarseness free" and ladies "upright in bearing, modest in behavior" are most welcome. The entrance inscription also invites those who preach "Christ's Holy Gospel" and adds this verse:

> Our Holy Writ and Word
> For ever shall be heard
> In this most holy spot.
> Each wears it on his heart,
> Each wears it as a sword,
> Our Holy Writ and Word.

Life is to be lived freely and pleasurably at Thélème, but clearly it is no fleshpot. It is a religious community where Christ's Gospel "for ever shall be heard." The Abbey is a paradisiacal ideal, no more realizable than More's utopian commonwealth, but like it a reflection, in large part satiric, on the life of its times and a critique of prevalent shortcomings and abuses. Those who are familiar with Erasmus' sharp critique of religious life in his day will recognize a Rabelaisian exaggeration of his point of view. I have also noted something more in ruminating on Rabelais' invention. It is reminiscent of the vision of the New Jerusalem "coming down out of heaven from God" that St. John describes in the twenty-first chapter of the book of Revelation. The structure of the Abbey and its adornment are similar to the holy city, though by no means identical. And similar too are the entrance restrictions. In the heavenly Jerusalem "nothing unclean shall enter, nor anyone whose ways are false or foul, but only those who are inscribed in the Lamb's roll of the living." Rabelais is equally exclusive. This similarity, if it be valid, bears out a thought I have about utopias: namely, that fundamentally they are related to a transcendant vision—"I saw new heavens and a new earth"—and are an adaptation of that vision, a mundane translation of it.

Michel de Montaigne comes next on our list. The utopia he describes is in his essay "On Cannibals."[3] It was published in 1580 in the first book of his *Essays*. Montaigne's account differs radically from the construct of both More and Rabelais, and there is no reason to think that he borrowed from his humanist forerunners. He harks back to a much older tradition. It is, however, a tale told to him by a traveler who had been to the New World and had lived there a number of years. He brings news to Montaigne of a "barbarous" people he had visited who "live very close to their original natural state." The laws of nature govern them, and they have not been corrupted by ours, Montaigne informs us. The initial approach and the very basic format are similar to More's: a traveler back from the New World reports the existence of a people living a well-nigh perfect life that is in sharp contrast to the wretched state of affairs in Europe. In fact, Montaigne regrets that Plato had no knowledge of this people, so superior is their natural way of life to the society he imagined in his *Republic*; and he declares:

> This is a nation, I should say to Plato, in which there is no sort of traffic: no knowledge of letters; no knowledge of numbers; no name for a magistrate, nor for political superiority; no custom of servitude, no riches or poverty, no contracts, no successions, no partitions, no occupations but leisure ones, no care for any but common kinship, no clothes, no agriculture, no metal, no use of wine or wheat. The very words that signify lying, treachery, dissimulation, avarice, envy, belittling, pardon are unheard of.

The description of this Garden of Eden I have just cited is a famous one. Shakespeare used it practically word for word in *The Tempest* from Florio's English translation of Montaigne's *Essays*. In Act II of the play Gonzalo, the old councilor to the king of Naples, describes in these same terms the commonwealth he would establish on the island where the royal party has been shipwrecked. Montaigne, however, gives many more details about the life of this primitive people. "The whole day is spent in dancing," he tells us, except, we must add, when the men are engaged in war. Valor in war and love for their wives are the two great moral principles that guide them. The chief duty of the wives, it would appear, is to keep their husbands' drink warm and seasoned. War plays an especially important role in their culture. It is a kind of lethal sport in which their courage is put to the supreme test. Surviving in battle, each brings home as a trophy the head of an enemy he has killed and/or a prisoner, if he is lucky, I presume, whom he will roast and eat with his friends. They are cannibals, as the title of the essay informs us. Montaigne is at pains to excuse or at least minimize this cannibalism. We do worse, he declares; we are blind to our own faults; "we surpass them in every kind of barbarism." He concludes that "there is an amazing distance between their character and our own."

How should we appraise this essay? It has two disparate parts, I think. One is the account of the "pure and simple naturalness" of that nation of "noble savages" who were found in the New World; the other is the story of their bloody warfare and their cannibalism. The former is a utopian vision with all the features of the classical Golden Age transposed to the newly discovered lands across the Atlantic; the latter is a tale hardly idyllic, hardly in keeping with the perfection of the natural state Montaigne so warmly praised. He has given us a picture of the "noble savage," but the burden of the essay is not simply that. He wants to open eyes and heighten awareness of the corruption at home, of the "barbarism" in civilized Europe, by a comparison that is shocking with the strange people, the cannibals he describes overseas. "I am not sorry that we notice the barbarous horror of [their] acts," Montaigne writes, "but I am sorry that while we judge their faults well we are so blind to our own." Insofar as the essay has this aim or intention it is similar in purpose to More's *Utopia*.

We can call Montaigne's "On Cannibals" a pivotal essay. It looks back to the Golden Age of ancient myth which Hesiod and Ovid and many others have described. Its features are the standard features of life in the primordial Golden Age. It was not difficult to attribute them to the seemingly uncivilized and unspoiled inhabitants of the New World. Travelers observed as much, and millennial dreams and hopes stirred many of the early Spanish missionaries there. The essay also looks forward to later versions of the "noble savage" concept, notably to Rousseau's view of the innocence and equality of man in nature as contrasted with his oppression and misery in organized society. The springs of Rousseau's radical revolt against the corrupt world he saw about him lay deep within, but he was influenced in his notion of the "natural man" and his goodness by the essay of Montaigne—the first part only, I am sure—that we have been considering. I have also read that Rousseau began to formulate his exalted view of man in nature as he meditated deep in the forest of Saint Germain-en-laye, a safe distance from the teeming misery of Paris. I must confess that I feel a kinship with him in this regard and share in his utopian reverie when I leave New York City and withdraw to the woods around my exurban home. Nature has that power.

Jonathan Swift came between Montaigne and Rousseau. But his utopia is quite another concept and a most unusual one. I am referring to the last voyage of Lemuel Gulliver in *Gulliver's Travels*, a work first published in 1726.[4] This voyage brought Gulliver to the country of the Houyhnhnms (pronounced Hwin-ums), that is, to an island inhabited by a race of horses who live by reason in pastoral peace and harmony with one another and who know neither falsehood nor any other vice. They "are endowed by Nature," Gulliver tells us, "with a general disposition to all virtues, and have no conceptions or ideas of what is evil in a rational creature, so their grand maxim is, to cultivate *Reason*, and to be wholly governed by it." Their very name, etymologically speaking, he relates, means "the Perfection of Nature," and so overwhelmed is Gulliver by their wisdom and goodness that he proposes them as models for mankind. Mankind in fact is seen in sharpest contrast to these marvelous quadrupeds. An unspeakably coarse and brutish breed of human-like creatures called Yahoos also live on the island and work as despised and despicable captives for the Houyhnhnms, but it is the more civilized race of humans back in England and Europe and their vicious ways and corrupt society that are excoriated by Swift in the account he presents and the contrast he so emphatically makes. There is a clear parallel here with Thomas More's *Utopia*, even though Swift's contrast is far more fantastic and his purpose broader and more scathing. His message is not quite the same. I also note some other parallels with More's construct. Both the Utopians and the Houyhnhnms are said to be governed by reason and to live in accordance with nature, and, most interestingly, the vice of pride is castigated in both books in a very special way. In *Utopia*, in its concluding pages, it is seen as the great vice, "the serpent from hell," which prevents men from building a better society. In *Gulliver's Travels*, in its final words, it is the evil Swift smites most severely and casts out. We know that Swift had great admiration for More. In *Gulliver's Travels* this is reflected in myriad ways.

Let us now turn to another eighteenth-century notable, a contemporary of Rousseau's, though a junior to Swift—in brief, to Voltaire. He did not share Rousseau's point of view or his political philosophy, though he was nevertheless a vigorous critic of the ills and follies of his day, and he sought change. Nor did he project a utopian vision. He was too realistic and hard-nosed. In his satiric novel *Candide*, however, he describes an idyllic kingdom which his hero Candide visits in his far-flung travels.[5] He calls it Eldorado, the Land of Gold—it was the name the Spaniards gave it—and it has all the earmarks of a utopia. Indeed, it has some of the character of Thomas More's Utopia. Candide's travels took him far and wide, and he suffered brutal and bizarre experiences every step of the way. His arrival in Eldorado begins the one happy interlude in his otherwise horrendous wanderings. In this remote country, high in the Andes, so it would seem, to which he came inadvertently with his servant Cacambo, he beheld a most agreeable land. He arrived first in a village where the children were playing at quoits, and to his amazement their rings were made of gold and precious stones. He reached an inn where a sumptuous meal was served him and no payment was asked. "Probably it is the country," observed Candide, "where everything is for the best; for there must be one country of that sort." Finally, he was taken to the capital city to meet the king, who received and entertained him with every favor.

There are many arresting features of life in Eldorado: the large red sheep that take the place of horses; the gold and precious gems that seem to abound—their "pebbles and mud," as the natives call them; the magnificence of the royal palace and the capital city. There are no law courts or prisons in Eldorado, for none are needed. Perhaps the most interesting part of Voltaire's description is Candide's inquiry about the religion of Eldorado. He is told by a wise old man: "We adore God from evening until morning. . . . He has given us everything, and we continually give him thanks." When asked about their priests the old man replies: "We are all priests; the king and heads of families solemnly sing praises every morning, accompanied by five or six thousand musicians." This exchange calls to mind Hythloday's discussion of the moral philosophy of the Utopians, though the latter is a more reasoned and extended analysis. But both, I believe, reinforce the view that it is good people who make a good society.

Candide should have stayed in Eldorado. Instead, after enjoying the hospitality of the king for a month, he asked leave to depart and take with him some of the "pebbles and mud" of the country. The king told him that the way out was very difficult, but that he would arrange to have him and his pack sheep hoisted over the high mountains that surround the kingdom. And so Candide left this utopia to resume his hazardous travels in the cruel world outside. He eventually found a haven "cultivating his garden" on a little farm in Turkey.

This brings us to the last author on the list, the Victorian poet and literary as well as social critic, Matthew Arnold. His is an odd name to link with the others I have been discussing, and his work, as impressive as it is, does not quite have the same character or reputation. He has, however, a utopian vision. It is different from those we have already seen, but it is an authentic one, I believe. I became aware of it not so long ago when I was reading Arnold's *Culture and Anarchy*, a work he first published in 1869—the same year Karl Marx published the first part of *Das Kapital*—and it is a work of political and social criticism, as its subtitle states.[6] In it Arnold addressed the unsettled and troubled state of England at that time, but his central argument can be abstracted, and it has, I think, a broader significance and a more general meaning than simply its application or relevance to the problems of its own contemporary scene.

The key word in Arnold's book and in his vision is the word *culture*. His essay, as he calls it, is the explanation of that term and how it can resolve the problems and remedy the faults of the England of his day. Let me quote his own words on his basic theme:

> The whole scope of the essay is to recommend culture as the great help out of our present difficulties: culture being a pur-

suit of our total perfection by means of getting to know, on all matters which most concern us, the best which has been thought and said in the world; and through this knowledge, turning a stream of fresh and free thought upon our stock notions and habits.[7]

In a similar vein he also declares: "Culture, which is the study of perfection, leads us . . . to conceive of true human perfection as a *harmonious* perfection, developing all sides of our humanity; and as a *general* perfection, developing all parts of our society."[8]

Arnold thus proposes culture as a personal and social ideal, and it is his constant association of the word *perfection* with it as well as his faith in its efficacy and attainment that have led me to view his proposal as embodying a utopian vision. His essay, of course, explains his concept of culture as the study and pursuit of human perfection more fully, and it applies this nostrum to specific ills and faults he observes in the political and social life of England. Liberal politicians, the Nonconformist mentality, middle-class Philistinism—all come under attack. He seeks, in short, an intellectual and moral enlightenment that will embrace and reform the nation. It is essentially an inward operation and achievement, but it will have a general expansion by virtue of what it is, and it will involve and be of benefit to all. It is a democratic social ideal.

How will this lofty aim, this high ideal be realized? Arnold eschews advocating any specific means or "machinery" in his essay, but it is obvious that the study and pursuit of our perfection, as he conceives it, must involve education in one way or another. It is basically a matter of acquiring knowledge, that is, of "getting to know . . . the best which has been thought and said in the world." It is clear that Arnold is in the great humanist tradition and that it is the study of the humanities on the broadest scale that he has in mind. John Henry Newman, whom he knew at Oxford, was a major influence on him, particularly in this case. One commentator on *Culture and Anarchy* has said that "but for Newman's *Idea of a University* it is likely that *Culture and Anarchy* would never have seen the light," and he continued: "when he [Arnold] speaks of 'culture' he is thinking of the 'liberal education' of which Newman writes made available for the whole of England by an indefinite multiplication of non-residential Rugby schools under state supervision."[9] These incisive words bring Arnold's program down to earth and spell out as concretely as one can what his lofty proposal is all about. They gain added force when one realizes that from 1851 until 1886, two years before his death, Arnold held the post of Her Majesty's Inspector of Schools. Few others in his day knew England and her educational, cultural, and social needs so well.

I come now to the peroration. We have examined ever so briefly a number of utopian visions, a number of very different utopian projections. They give rise both individually and jointly to a host of issues and questions. Thomas More's *Utopia*, that deeply "enigmatic book," as it has been called, in particular is inexhaustible in that regard, but each one— each book, each name mentioned—can stimulate our minds and occupy our thoughts for a long time. But, this survey completed, are there any general observations that I can make? Two spring to mind. The first is that all the visions or projections I have described, all six of them, appear to demonstrate that a good society or community depends on having good people to make and maintain it. There is a famous line in Thomas More's *Utopia* where he says "it is impossible that all should be well unless all men were good," and he adds immediately, "a situation which I do not expect for a great many years to come." That's a profound comment on the utopian ideal. More has stated clearly, it seems to me, the great prerequisite, the *sine qua non*, for any state or any place that would be perfect or nearly so. In Montaigne's essay, in the first part at least (and with Rousseau), it is assumed that man by nature and in the natural state is good.

With Matthew Arnold it is assumed that education can make him so, that is, that education, the right education, can develop our full potential and render us "perfect." The other four utopias are already inhabited by good people, or in the case of Swift by good quadrupeds. The question that arises in these cases is "What has made them good?" or more universally "What makes people good?" The answer to this query, I think, will take us to the essential problem, the very crux of the utopian idea. I shall leave the thought for you to wrestle with.

My other observation is related, I believe. It is that the utopian phenomenon is linked to a transcendent vision, that is, to our religious consciousness. I mentioned this earlier when I was discussing Rabelais' Abbey of Thélème. But it seems fairly obvious in that case.[10] In the others, I would say, it springs from even a deeper source, from that striving for perfection which arises naturally from the depths of the human heart. And in one idiom or another we all pray "Thy kingdom come" and in our innermost being desire that realization.

Notes

1. I explain this more fully in chap. 4 above, "Erasmus' *Adagia* and More's *Utopia.*"
2. *The History of Gargantua and Pantagruel,* trans. J. M. Cohen (Baltimore, 1955), pp. 149–60.
3. In *The Essential Montaigne,* trans. Serge Hughes (New York, 1970), pp. 264–76.
4. (London, 1985), Part IV.
5. *Candide, or Optimism,* trans. Richard Aldington, ed. Norman L. Torrey (New York, 1946), pp. 52–61.
6. Ed. J. Dover Wilson (Cambridge, 1960).

7. Ibid., p. 6.
8. Ibid., p. 11.
9. Ibid., p. xiv.
10. See John 8:31–34 and Gal. 6:1. Is this the source of Rabelais' invention?

6

The Jesuits, Humanism, and History

In memoriam Gerald M. Quinn

MY TITLE IS BROADLY DESCRIPTIVE of the three topics I intend to discuss. The terms need clarification, and this and the thoughts that spring therefrom will be the burden of practically all I have to say. A subtitle I had originally appended, "Quincentennial Reflections," indicates the occasion and character of my remarks. We celebrated in 1991 the 500th anniversary of the birth of Saint Ignatius Loyola. It was indeed a time to reflect on his legacy or on a significant aspect of it, on its historical actuality as well as on its relevance and meaning today. I felt entitled to do so. I was a student of the Jesuits in my youth and college years. I taught in Jesuit schools nearly all my adult life. I have been an historian of Ignatius and his times. I am not a Jesuit, but I have certainly been influenced by them, and over the course of the years many of my friends have belonged to the Society Saint Ignatius founded. I am not a stranger to the subject at hand.

My three topics are interrelated. I am interested in knowing how the early Jesuits fit into the picture of Renaissance humanism and then more specifically what part, if any, history played in the Jesuit culture I shall discuss. Finally, I want to relate these matters of historic interest to our own scene today. But first, the triad. The notion of the Jesuits is unambiguous, but the concept of humanism and the meaning of history in this context have to be explained. Let me take up this triad in orderly sequence.

The story of the Society of Jesus begins with the Spanish soldier, the caballero, whose quincentenary we were celebrating. He was badly wounded in a battle with the French at Pamplona in Navarre in 1521 and experienced a religious conversion during the time of his convalescence. He decided to go off as a pilgrim to Jerusalem as soon as he was able. Iñigo Lopez de Loyola, such was his name, set out from his home in the Basque country of northern Spain the following year. He crossed Spain, visited the shrine of Our Lady at Montserrat in Catalonia, and stayed several months in the nearby town of Manresa. Finally, by way of Rome and Venice he made the journey to the Holy Land. He was not permitted to remain there as he had intended, and disappointed and uncertain about his future course he returned to Barcelona. He now decided to study, he tells us in his *Autobiography*, so that he might be able "to help souls." A long and rather checkered academic period now followed. After some Latin instruction in Barcelona he went to the university at Alcalá de Henares in central Spain which Cardinal Ximenes de Cisneros had established less than twenty years before and then to Salamanca, the site of Spain's oldest university. Finally, he came to Paris to study in early 1528, and he obtained his Master of Arts there in 1534. He also studied theology for a short time with the Dominicans in Paris. Ignatius was not a brilliant scholar or a great intellectual, but he devoted time and energy to acquiring a good education. We might also note he was well beyond the age for a university student: he was in his mid-forties when he finished in Paris.

Strangely enough, after completing the studies he had pursued so long he was determined to return to the Holy Land to evangelize the Moslems. He and several companions, younger students whom he had met at the university in Paris, vowed to do so in the summer of 1534. A few years later this band—there were now ten in all—gathered in Venice to find passage to the East. Because of war that had broken out with the Turks they were unable to do so, and in early 1538

Saint Ignatius Loyola, fresco by Andrea Pozzo, ca. 1685. Discovered during restoration of Saint Ignatious' rooms at the Gesù, Rome.

they went to Rome and offered their services to the Pope. This was Paul III, the Farnese Pope, whose pontificate marks a critical turning point in the history of the Catholic Church. Ignatius and his friends had come to a Rome where the forces for renewal and reform were slowly gaining strength. In these circumstances their unheralded arrival is an event of historic importance, for very shortly they will play a major part in the Catholic revival that was now beginning. In Rome they organized more formally as a religious community and won papal approval. The Society of Jesus had now come into being. The official bull of institution, *Regimini militantis ecclesiae*, was issued in September 1540.

The Society grew very rapidly. New members joined immediately, the companions dispersed on various missions at the behest of the Pope, Ignatius alone of the original band staying in Rome to direct the fast growing order. He was chosen its head or general and remained such up to his death on July 31, 1556. By that time there were some 1,000 members in the new order laboring in every part of the world. By that time too the Society had become a major educational force in Catholic Europe. It had established over thirty colleges for lay students in eight countries, and many more were in the offing. There were approximately 245 such colleges by the end of the century, and the Society itself numbered close to 10,000 members. Education unquestionably had become one of the Society's chief occupations, and it continued to be one of the most important and characteristic features of the Society's worldwide apostolate. How did this happen? How did the experience and intentions of a Spanish soldier who wanted to live and work among the Moslems evolve into so extensive and intensive an educational enterprise? It certainly was not the normal or traditional undertaking for a religious order. As we ponder it, the more unusual, even paradoxical, this development appears. It presents an intriguing problem to the historian. Let me offer an explanation.

Ignatius lived, studied, participated, undertook his religious mission, and with his youthful friends founded the Society of Jesus in a Europe in the full flush of expansion, change, and crisis. These were the climactic years of the period we often refer to as the Renaissance and Reformation, code words that signify an awakening, expanding, changing world marked by great intellectual and religious ferment. Ignatius would have been dull and insentient indeed if he had not been affected by the events of his day and by the currents that swirled about him in the 1520s and 1530s when he was pursuing his university education. Many events and currents spring to mind: the expansion of Spain, the worldwide discoveries and explorations, the Turkish threat, the Protestant revolt, the crisis in the Church, the invention and rapid expansion of printing, the New Learning, as it is called. This last-mentioned cultural and intellectual movement which has also been labeled humanism was especially important and pervasive in Europe in Ignatius' time, and my thesis is that he as well as his friends and other early Jesuits were deeply influenced by it. This influence, I believe, goes far in explaining the origin and the character of the educational enterprise the Society of Jesus so early undertook.[1] It does not tell us the whole story of Ignatius and the Jesuits, but it tells us a lot.

To clarify and give credence to this view it is necessary first of all to explain what humanism in the Renaissance context actually means. The word itself, as Fowler's dictionary observes, "is apt to puzzle or mislead." It has been used in recent times to signify a totally secular, even atheist, attitude or philosophy. That meaning is far removed from its Renaissance connotation and use. But even here there has been a great deal of misunderstanding and confusion about what the term covers or implies. This has been due to erroneous notions about the Renaissance and its culture: notions that the classical revival of the Renaissance was marked by a kind of reversion to paganism and was antithetic to Christian faith and morals (Burckhardt's great classic helped lead us down that path), and notions, for example, that Erasmus, the prince of humanists, was skeptical and irreligious, a Voltaire of the sixteenth century. These notions had been fairly commonplace until a short time ago, and they still linger as rather formless popular views which textbooks and the media continue to exploit. Among historians, however, there has been a major revision of these notions in recent years all along the line, a revision that amounts to a complete reversal almost of the earlier views.[2]

I will not belabor this important historiographical development. But the new understanding about the Renaissance and its culture bears directly on my thesis that Ignatius and the early Jesuits were influenced by humanism. How, then, should we understand the term? It is the word we use to signify the great interest in and the study of the classical languages and literature at the time of the Renaissance. It was a scholarly and educational movement, and it stressed that an education based on the ancient classics and modeled on the curriculum of Roman antiquity was the proper training for an individual, given his or her human nature, capacity, and social role. Latin and Greek, grammar and rhetoric, the ancient authors were its mainstay—in fact, its content. These constituted the *litterae humaniores* or *studia humanitatis*, that is, the letters or studies most beneficial and useful in view of our humanity. From this concept and terminology our words "humanism" and "humanities" are derived. In Ignatius' time this humanism, which had its origin in the Italy of the Renaissance, was sweeping Europe. It was the New Learning, and it was aggressively challenging and upsetting older patterns of thought and education. Every land had its humanist scholars and centers of study. The latter were especially the trilingual colleges that began to appear in the early sixteenth century. The first of these was the college of San Ildefonso which Cardinal Ximenes had established at Alcalá de Henares in Spain. The printing press too was multiplying texts and treatises which fostered the movement. The works of Erasmus, especially, circulated widely in the early sixteenth century in the promotion and defense of good learning and classical letters.

We must underscore that humanism had a very dynamic reform thrust. The humanists believed that the revival of letters, the *litterae humaniores*, and an education based thereon would produce a better and more enlightened person and that social improvement would follow. They linked the education and learning they espoused to good behavior and to religious and social reform. They were moralists and reformers to the core. Erasmus is the great name here, but many others shared his views and aims. Thomas More's *Utopia*, which was published in 1516, for example, clearly manifests this relationship of good learning, the right values, and social reform. Nor should one think for a moment that there is something antithetic to Christian principles or orthodoxy in this humanism. The humanists were Christian humanists, and they followed a patristic tradition which justified the cultivation and use of classical letters. In fact, a scriptural and patristic revival became an integral part of the humanist movement by the sixteenth century, and some very notable work which had been pioneered earlier by Italian scholars was accomplished in this field. Cardinal Ximenes' great polyglot Bible is a prime example. It was published at Alcalá just a few years before Ignatius arrived there in 1526. Again Erasmus' contributions here are landmark events.

My point here is not only that Ignatius could not have been oblivious to all of this but also that he was influenced by the movement I have described. His decision to pursue an education when he returned from the Holy Land in 1524 points in that direction and sets him on that course. Going to Alcalá soon after was an interesting choice. He was there only briefly, but there are intriguing aspects to his stay. For one thing he became acquainted with and had close ties with the family of a printer there, Miguel de Eguia, who in 1526 published a Spanish translation of Erasmus' *Enchiridion militis christiani*. Ignatius most likely read the work at that time, and we can trace its influence on him. I discussed this at some length in a paper I gave and an article I wrote quite a few years ago.[3] Harassed by the Inquisition, however, Ignatius moved on to Salamanca and then out of Spain entirely to Paris. The Paris years are most important. He began his studies at the College of Montaigu and then in the fall of 1529 shifted to the College of Sainte-Barbe where he eventually completed his Master of Arts. This shift is very significant. Ignatius moved from a conservative stronghold, one associated with an anti-humanist and anti-Erasmian point of view, to one thoroughly penetrated by the new humanism. All the university had felt the impact of the New Learning, but Sainte-Barbe in particular espoused and expounded the classical program. Ignatius' academic training occurred under its auspices, as did that of his young companions with whom he was to form the Society of Jesus. After their studies in Paris, as I have said, they proceeded to carry out their vow to go to Jerusalem and "spend their lives in the service of souls," in Ignatius' words. War made this impossible, and so they went to Rome and put themselves at the disposal of the Pope.

New and unexpected developments now quickly followed. It is a remarkable and eventful story that unfolds. The only aspects of it I want to stress are (1) the education and training of the young Jesuits now entering the order, and (2) the establishment of the colleges where the Society undertook to educate others. These are two closely related aspects, two sides of the same coin. The coin is humanism. As they saw the need and importance of a solid education in the humanist vein for themselves, so they saw its value for others. And as they had received such an education themselves, so they were able to offer it to others. The one led to the other in a natural sequence, given the reform thrust of the humanist ideal. Let us look at them separately for the moment.

Ignatius insisted that new members entering the Society be given the same kind of education that he and his friends had received in Paris. The *modus et ordo parisiensis* and the humanist program of Sainte-Barbe thus became the model to be followed.[4] In the very beginning new student members of the Society were sent to Paris for their schooling. In 1542 there was a community of sixteen Jesuits living and studying there, but war which broke out between France and Spain that year caused its dispersal. Seven Spaniards in the group shifted to Louvain where they continued their studies at the trilingual college whose foundation in 1517 was due to Erasmus. An important community of Jesuits was established at Louvain which in turn attracted some new and outstanding members from the Low Countries. At the same time three Portuguese Jesuit students moved from Paris to Coimbra in Portugal where the university had recently been re-established and reformed under the auspices of King John III, an ardent patron of the New Learning. A Jesuit community and house of study was soon established there and endowed by the king, and it grew rapidly to become the principal house of the early Society. By 1546 there were 80 students there. I have been particularly interested in the early Jesuits at Coimbra, and a number of years ago I had a Gulbenkian grant to do research in Portugal on their presence at this university center and their ties with humanism and reform there. My inquiry was a sequel in a sense to the study of Erasmus and St. Ignatius I referred to above. It was not extensive, but I was struck by the circumstances and connections I perceived. These first Jesuits had entered a very active educational and religious reform scene, and from the start they shared and participated in it. They attended classes at the university, which had absorbed some earlier trilingual schools. This development was climaxed by the founding of a royal College of Arts in 1548, a school that was turned over to the Jesuits in 1555. The role of John III in support both of humanist reform and of the early Society is most impressive, and the connections of Sainte-Barbe in Paris with these events in Portugal are quite remarkable. Ignatius and his friends had attended Sainte-Barbe, of course, but the Portuguese king had also funded scholarships at Sainte-Barbe, and other scholars and professors from that college played a part in the reforms at Coimbra.[5]

These early groups of Jesuits studying at Paris or Louvain or Coimbra or other universities formed the original colleges of the Society. They were residences or houses of study for members of the new order. When and how did Ignatius and his confrères become engaged in educating others? The transition, as we have indicated, was a natural one. As early as 1539 Paul III had asked two of the founder members of the new order, Peter Faber and Diego Lainez, to teach theology at the Sapienza, the papal college in Rome, and in 1543 Francis Xavier, who was now beginning his great missionary work in the East, reported from Goa in India that some members were teaching the humanities as well as Christian doctrine there. In 1545 Francis Borgia, the Duke of Gandia in Spain and later a member of the Society himself, endowed a school for the training of young Jesuits at Gandia, and there the following year some classes were opened to students who were not members of the new order. The major step, however, was the opening of a college for lay students or externs, as they are called, at Messina in Sicily in 1548. This was the first Jesuit school that offered an education to the public at large, and it is the prototype of all other Jesuit colleges. Its foundation marks the beginning of the vast Jesuit educational enterprise.

It came about in the following way. The city fathers of Messina wrote Ignatius to ask that he send ten members of his order to teach and preach among them. "Our request," they wrote, "is that you send us five masters to teach theology, the arts, rhetoric, and grammar, and another five to pursue their studies and give assistance in works of Christian zeal." Ignatius agreed, and without delay he selected and dispatched ten of his best for the task. The group was headed by a brilliant scholar from Paris who had known Ignatius there and who several years later had come to Rome to join the Society. His name is Jerome Nadal. He is one of the most important members of the early Society and the founder of its educational system. He became rector of the college that was formally opened that October. The group also included Peter Canisius, the first German Jesuit, and several others all educated in the humanist vein. The curriculum they designed and began to teach unmistakably bears this stamp. The school at Messina was a trilingual college, and it adopted the *modus et ordo parisiensis*. Latin, Greek, and Hebrew were taught. An orderly progression or *ascensus* through grammar classes to classes in the humanities and then in rhetoric followed. Nearly all the great Latin and Greek authors were read and studied: Cicero, Virgil, Ovid, Horace, Aesop, Homer, Aristophanes, Lucian, and in rhetoric above all Quintilian's *Institutio oratoria*. Works of contemporary humanists were also used: those of Erasmus, Vives, Lorenzo Valla. Three texts of Erasmus appear by name: his *De copia verborum ac rerum*, his *De conscribendis epistolis*, and a work on Latin syntax, *De constructione*. The college at Messina and its *ratio studiorum* could not have been more humanistic.

The school was most successful. The following year the citizens of Palermo appealed to Ignatius to send them some Jesuit teachers to establish a similar school in their city. Ignatius agreed, and in November 1549 the second Jesuit college for externs was formally opened. Other requests were also arriving. For guidance Ignatius asked Nadal to send him a complete description of Messina's program. This was dispatched to Rome in July 1551 in an account by a professor of the humanities at Messina, Hannibal du Coudret, and it in turn became the blueprint for the Roman college which Ignatius established that year. He intended this college both for externs and for selected young Jesuit students who would be trained there to teach in the other colleges the Society would establish. It was to become the center and the model for the educational network that was being built.

The development I have traced is an amazing one. It carries us from the conversion of a Spanish soldier in 1521 and his pilgrimage to Jerusalem to the establishment of hundreds of schools in Europe and beyond based solidly on the New Learning of the Renaissance. The explanation for this, as I have stressed, lies above all in the impact and influence of humanism on Ignatius and his fellow Jesuits. Viewed in this light their educational apostolate is one of the great extensions and consolidations of Renaissance humanism. The historical significance of this can hardly be exaggerated.

I stand in awe too of the fact that this Jesuit enterprise has continued on a worldwide scale down to my own day. In describing it I feel that I have told the story of my own roots. *De me fabula narratur.* I attended a Jesuit high school and college many years ago when the old *ratio studiorum* was still in force. There had been changes in the *ratio*, to be sure, since the sixteenth century, and our classical studies perhaps were not as rigorous or as comprehensive as in the early days at Messina or the Roman college. Our humanism, I think, was somewhat attenuated. We were among the students of the final days. But I studied Latin and Greek, followed substantially the Messina program, and was instructed and trained in the tradition of the *modus et ordo parisiensis.* My tie with this historic past thus is intimate and real, and its influence on me, I know, is profound. I am quite overwhelmed by this historical reality and amused too, I must confess, at how fortuitous the encounter was back there in Buffalo, New York, and how unintended and how unaware I was of its true character. It was real enough though, and as I look back on it thoughts about its meaning and relevance today inevitably arise.

Before I get into a discussion of that thorny question, however, let me turn to the third topic of the triad I planned to explore, that is, the role of history in the context of the early Jesuits and humanism. I originally included it because of my interest in the subject of humanism and history, but I soon came to realize that it involves a factor of great importance in understanding the early Jesuits and their achievement and in analyzing their potential and course of action today. The topic is not as clear-cut as the other two I have discussed, however. For one thing the notion of history can be understood in several different ways: history as the past, history as a narrative of past events, history as a discipline or subject for study, and, by extension, history as an attitude toward the past, an awareness about the course of human events.

In Ignatius' time history was not an academic discipline or subject, but as a narrative of events it was a form of knowledge, a *scientia*, and a branch of literature. And there were, of course, Roman and Greek historians, as there were Renaissance ones. The humanists, following classical models, saw history as coming under the aegis of rhetoric and as having a didactic function. It was the *magistra vitae*, and it should be written with skill and eloquence. These requirements by no means ruled out a critical approach or the desire to uncover the truth. Cicero in the *De oratore*, for example, had written that the first law of history was to tell the truth. Style, purpose, truthfulness were all of its essence. I came to appreciate this view of the matter as I worked on Erasmus' monumental edition of the writings of Saint Jerome and translated his life of the saint which served as an introduction to his edition. Erasmus wrote a critical and well-documented life of Jerome which also had a definite rhetorical character and which shared in his basic aim to reform theology.[6] In the opening section of the life he also set down the critical standards that would guide him in his narrative, and he produced a remarkable statement on historical method which, I think, is unique in the literature of that time.

I will not attempt to analyze early Jesuit historical writing in these humanist terms. What there is of it is confined to histories of the society and lives of Saint Ignatius, of which Pedro Ribadeneira's, published in 1572, was the first. But mentioning Erasmus' life of Saint Jerome calls to mind the great enterprise in historical research which a number of Belgian Jesuits began in the seventeenth century. I refer to the Bollandists, as they are known, and their project of critically editing the lives of the saints, an enormous project which has produced the famous *Acta sanctorum* and is still being carried on. The early Jesuits, I am sure, were in accord with the humanist view of history, and a critical approach like Erasmus' would not have been foreign to them. In their early colleges the ancient historians were read as part of the *litterae humaniores* which was the whole basis of the education they offered. Ignatius himself in the *Constitutions of the Society* (Part IV, chap. XII, A) included history along with grammar, rhetoric, and poetry in explaining the *litterae humaniores*. At the college at Messina and the Roman college the earliest documents mention Sallust, Livy, Suetonius, and Thucydides as being prescribed particularly in the rhetoric class. Nadal a little later in an *ordo studiorum* recommended that professors in the humanities and rhetoric classes explain the rules of historical narrative and have the students compose a brief history in Latin. Still later some discussion did arise about having a course in history, but the original *ratio studiorum* never conceded that and in the early period at least history remained a subordinate part of a solidly classical curriculum.[7]

One other aspect of history that I referred to particularly intrigues me—the aspect that involves an historical attitude or consciousness, that is, a sense of history. Humanism by definition embodies such, and its whole scholarly procedure in the broad sense consists of an historical method. It is clearly marked by a perspective on the past, and the learning of the ancient languages and the recovery and study of ancient texts are the means whereby that past will be known and its culture restored. The Jesuits being humanists certainly had this frame of mind, that is, they had a perspective on history and possessed a sense of history. I believe we see this reflected not only in their humanism but in all they did—in their manifold activity in the changing and tumultuous world they lived in and in their many ventures both as individuals and as a dynamic religious order. Their dynamism perhaps was in large part the result of this historical awareness. This is a subject that can certainly be further and very fruitfully explored. But let me offer one case that may help clarify or substantiate what I mean. Saint Ignatius toward the end of his life dictated a short autobiography at the instance of Nadal and other colleagues.[8] It is the story of his conversion and spiritual growth. It is personal history in the richest sense of the word: his religious experience is placed graphically in the context of events, and the account he gives conveys a keen awareness of historical circumstance and of his movement and development in its midst. It exudes a sense of history. I rank it together with Erasmus' life of Saint Jerome, which indeed is a very different kind of life, among the greatest and most instructive of Renaissance biographies.

That brings me to the question of the meaning and relevance today of this Jesuit humanism. The historical perceptiveness of Ignatius and the early Jesuits of which I have just been speaking opened their minds, I believe, to the attraction and influence of humanism, and that movement contributed its share to their historical awareness. Humanism was pivotal in this regard; it was an effect as well as cause of their sense of history. But the point I want to make is that the humanism of the early Jesuits and their educational apostolate was in tune with the times and with the best and most progressive current of the times.[9] It entailed an acceptance of high cultural and intellectual standards; it was a response to pressing needs—the need for an educated priesthood, the need for cultural and religious renewal, the need for educational reform. Times indeed have changed since that early period of their foundation and incredible expansion. What was fit and proper for those earlier times is not necessarily the case today.

Our world is so totally different and more complicated and fragmented. Science and technology, high-tech technology, are paramount, secular concerns dominate, social problems abound, very different standards and values, if these terms can even be used, prevail. It is hardly surprising that the classics of Rome and Greece that had been the heart of the Jesuit *ratio studiorum* have been abandoned. This departure from past and long-lived tradition has been recent, but it should not really perplex us as we look at the chaotic and troubled world about us. Not to adapt to current needs and conditions and therefore to change is to die. The law of life is change, and the Jesuits obviously have adapted to the radically different circumstances of the world today. A variety of reasons are at work here, but certainly the historical perceptiveness and awareness which I have attributed to the sons of Saint Ignatius dictated it. That same sense of history, I expect, can be a guide and support in the changes that must occur.

A recent comment by Father Kolvenbach, the Superior General of the Society, gives some indication of one aspect of those changes. Permit me to quote it here:

> I am convinced that in 400 years of history our educational institutions have had as their sole end the commitment to make the human city a more just one for the Lord's sake. I am anxious to emphasize this since, when we Jesuits declare that today we are called to promote justice and to live the option for the poor, we are not formulating a new response; it is rather a new way of expressing an old response, well anchored in our Jesuit traditions. We have never been satisfied with mere cultural transmission. We have always insisted on developing a critical attitude, to equip our students to contribute to humane and cultural growth and to renewal in harmony with Gospel values.[10]

The idiom and indeed the content of Father Kolvenbach's remarks are unmistakably modern. Do they translate or echo the earlier humanism of the *ratio studiorum*? Not explicitly perhaps at first hearing, but given the reform thrust of humanism and the very different context today they represent, I think, an adaptation of the Society's educational apostolate—"a new way of expressing an old response, well anchored in our Jesuit traditions," as Father Kolvenbach so well explained it. Nor is the promotion of social justice an alien concept in humanism (I have touched on this). Indeed we have Thomas More's *Utopia* to disprove such a notion, and we have the Jesuit-sponsored and -directed Indian communities in South America, the Paraguay Reductions, as ample reminders of a linkage here and a root tradition. I can also testify from my own experience in the old days of the classical *ratio studiorum* that the concerns that Father Kolvenbach voiced were never absent and in their own way at that earlier date inspired thought and action. The task now, it would seem, is how to implement in today's world more fully and effectively the goal and commitment which Father Kolvenbach expressed.

From another and very different perspective let me also comment on the kind of adaptation that is required. There are two fundamental features of humanist education that are enduring, I believe, and that should be borne in mind and should inform whatever changes or reforms in our educational systems we seek to achieve today. One is that humanism has a moral dimension and that education in the *litterae humaniores* was linked to the formation of character and the inculcation of virtue. "No man can be an orator unless he is a good man," Quintilian declares, and in the twelfth book of his *Institutio oratoria* he is at great pains to expand and explain that essential concept. Classical literature was meant to enlighten and inspire, and the very language itself was intended to elevate and ennoble. This brings me to the other feature of humanism that should be retained. The cultivation of eloquence, that is the ability to speak and write well, was a prime focus or goal in humanist education. This *ars humanitatis*, as it was called (the term speaks volumes), in turn was linked to the cultivation of our mind, the development of our intellect, for thought and speech were deemed inseparable. The Greek word *logos*, for instance, stood for both. Cardinal Newman expressed this perfectly in a splendid passage in a lecture on literature that is appended to his *Idea of a University*:

> Thought and speech are inseparable from each other. Matter and expression are parts of one: style is a thinking out into language. This is what I have been laying down, and this is literature: not *things*, not the verbal symbols of things; not on the other hand mere *words*; but thoughts expressed in language.

These two fundamental features of humanist education, and of what has generally been recognized as a liberal education, in some way we have to render anew. The preservation of a civilized and humane culture and of human values, I think, depends upon it. We are aware of this today, and, as we know, there has been a great deal of discussion about this in recent years.[11] A widespread perception prevails that something is seriously lacking in the higher education we impart and that a crisis in the liberal arts, if not in our fundamental moral and cultural assumptions, is at hand. The problem is seen basically as a failure to affirm values, to search out what is true, the very notion of which is questioned, and to train the mind so that it can attain what Newman called "a connected view or grasp of things." Yet it can hardly be denied that virtue, vision, and *veritas*, to sum up our cause alliteratively, are basic human needs and that we fail and founder when we ignore this necessity and spurn their pursuit.

We can expostulate at length on this. Our terms may be subject to some debate, but most will agree that the absence of what they signify entails serious consequences for society as well as for the individual. We know that there is a distinction between virtue and vice; "Where there is no vision the people perish" is an age-old proverb we continue to believe; and Simone Weil's declaration that "the need of truth is more sacred than any other need" does not strike us as hyperbole. The question is how to make our educational systems respond to the basic needs we perceive and accomplish the goals we desire.

Unquestionably there are problems here—practical problems, personnel problems, cultural problems, problems related to strongly held view and divergent opinions, problems posed by vested interests. Also, the need for skills, for technical, vocational, and professional training, and for useful and scientific knowledge cannot be minimized or overlooked. Indeed, improvement in this area is constantly sought. Yet this cannot be the sole purpose of education. Few question this at least in theory. Difficulties and disagreements arise when one moves further along into the real world of application and administration. Unfortunately I have no concrete solutions to offer. I have simply reached this point in my essay as a result of my reflections on Jesuit humanism and the traditional *ratio studiorum*. Their relevance today inevitably arose, and I sketched out certain aims and ideals inherent in this humanist Jesuit tradition that should serve as an inspiration and guide for the reforms we might undertake. Can I say more?

Actually I have said a great deal, but it has been on the level of guiding principles rather than of implementation or adaptation. But this is important, and my concluding words will only be reiterative. Social justice, moral formation, intellectual development as basic educational goals must be kept foremost in mind and must consciously inform the changes we make. We must at the same time realistically appraise contemporary needs and demands. I shall let others spell this out. My focus has been on the Jesuit example and the legacy they have left us. It would be a tragedy to ignore or disavow it.

Notes

1. On this influence see also John W. O'Malley, s.j., "Renaissance Humanism and the Religious Culture of the First Jesuits," *The Heythrop Journal*, 31 (1990), 471–87, and "Was Ignatius Loyola a Church Reformer: How to Look at Early Modern Catholicism," *The Catholic Historical Review*, 77 (1991), 182–83. Note especially Father O'Malley's recent *The First Jesuits* (Cambridge, Mass., 1993).

2. See, for example, Charles Trinkaus, *In Our Image and Likeness: Humanity and Divinity in Italian Humanist Thought*, 2 vols. (Chicago, 1970). As for Erasmus, see my "Interpreting Erasmus," in *Six Essays on Erasmus* (New York, 1979), chap. 5, pp. 57–73.

3. "Erasmus and St. Ignatius Loyola," in *Six Essays on Erasmus*, chap. 6, pp. 75–92.

4. On early Jesuit education and the first colleges, see Allan P. Farrell, s.j., *The Jesuit Code of Liberal Education* (Milwaukee, 1938), and Gabriel Codina Mir, s.j., *Aux sources de la pédagogie des Jésuits: Le 'modus parisiensis'* (Rome, 1968).

5. Elisabeth F. Hirsch, "Erasmus and Portugal," *Bibliothèque d'humanisme et renaissance*, 32 (1970), 539–57, is informative on this theme.

6. See my "*Eloquentia, Eruditio, Fides*: Erasmus' *Life of Jerome*," in *Acta Conventus Neo-Latini Sanctandreani*, ed. I. D. McFarlane (Binghamton, N.Y., 1986), pp. 269–74. The English translation of the *Life* is in CWE 61, pp. 15–62. See also pp. 11–14 above.

7. See Farrell, *Jesuit Code of Liberal Education*, pp. 247–51.

8. *The Autobiography of St. Ignatius Loyola*, trans. Joseph F. O'Callaghan, ed. John C. Olin (New York, 1992).

9. It is a point also well made in the opening pages of George E. Ganss, s.j., *Saint Ignatius' Idea of a Jesuit University* (Milwaukee, 1954).

10. I quote this from an interview with Father Kolvenbach that appeared in *America*, September 29, 1990.

11. Allan Bloom's widely read *The Closing of the American Mind* (New York, 1987) springs to mind, as does an even more specific

critique of the shortcomings of higher education today: Page Smith's *Killing the Spirit: Higher Education in America* (New York, 1990). The titles of both books indicate their concern and alarm. The subject itself is not entirely new. Bloom's predecessor at The University of Chicago Robert Maynard Hutchins raised some of the same issues in his book *The Higher Learning in America* back in 1936, and Hutchins' stress on the training of the mind and the pursuit of truth as basic in a liberal education harks back to Cardinal Newman's classic work. The most recent phase of the discussion, at least from media accounts, appears to be a sterile debate between what very loosely (and not very informatively) is called Western culture or the Western tradition and an angry "multiculturalism" focusing on issues of gender and race. If nothing more, it is indicative of the depths we have reached in discussing these important matters and is symptomatic perhaps of serious social and cultural disorder.

www.ingramcontent.com/pod-product-compliance
Lightning Source LLC
Chambersburg PA
CBHW031255290426
44109CB00012B/588